THE

COUNSELLOR'S

TOOLKIT

COUPLES COUNSELLING THROUGH A MENTAL HEALTH LENS

Oliver de Nicolai

DISCLAIMER

The information provided in this book is for educational and informational purposes only and does not constitute professional, clinical, or legal advice. The examples and vignettes throughout are illustrative composites drawn from the author's professional experience. They do not depict any single client, couple, or case. Every effort has been made to ensure that identifying details have been altered or omitted to protect confidentiality.

While care has been taken to ensure the accuracy of the content at the time of publication, readers are encouraged to exercise their own professional judgement and seek supervision or additional guidance where appropriate. The author and publisher disclaim all liability for any direct or indirect consequences arising from the use or interpretation of the material contained herein.

CONTENTS

DEDICATION

This book is for the counsellors who sit outside a couples' session thinking, *"What if I get it wrong? What if I can't help them? What if they start arguing about bins again and I freeze?"*

It's for those who care so much about their clients that the thoughts don't quiet down until long after the session ends. For those who lie awake at night replaying conversations, wishing they'd asked one more question or paused just a little longer.

It's for the new counsellors who walk into the room with their heart in their throat, secretly wondering if they're cut out for this, and then discover — often in the middle of a messy argument about dishwashers — that their presence alone makes a difference.

It's for the peers who offer insights in supervision, sometimes profound, sometimes hilarious, but always reminding us that we're not in this alone. Peers who say, "I've been there," and mean it.

It's for the brave counsellors who show up as themselves — authentic, curious, human — even when they don't feel particularly wise. Because in those moments, clients see not a perfect professional but a steady companion.

And, of course, it's for the couples. The ones who argue, laugh, despair, and hope. The ones who teach us, session after session, that relationships are both fragile and resilient, both ordinary and extraordinary. Thank you for trusting us with your stories.

To all of you — this book is my way of saying: you are enough, you are not alone, and the work you do matters more than you know.

FOREWORD

Counsellors often shy away for couples counselling for many reasons. There is much less emphasis on couples work during training, and it can seem incredibly daunting to hold the space for a couple in conflict or crisis. There is a tension in the air that is not present when counselling individuals. We bear witness to the hurt and grief that comes with a relationship breakdown. Relationships are hard. Love can hurt. On occasion we wear the blame if the relationship cannot repair, but we continue to hold space for the grief that comes with letting go.

However, we also get to watch the joy that comes when couples find each other again. With baby steps we watch the walls crack, see the small steps towards vulnerability. We get to share the relief and the ecstasy of reconnection. So, the work can be immensely satisfying, which is what keeps us in this field.

I met Oliver around five years ago when he reached out to me to meet for a coffee. We had both set up private practice a few hundred meters from each other on a fashionable café strip in a leafy Brisbane suburb. Oliver's quirky sense of humour, and his genuine authenticity disarms. We have never felt in competition with each other. Instead, we refer clients to each other. This speaks to his generosity of spirit and his genuine wish to help others in the industry.

Oliver's Couples Toolkit is a beautifully written, gentle companion for us. Just as we remind our clients to pause, to give space to feelings, and that we are enough, Oliver reminds us as counsellors to do the same. That it is not our job to fix the crisis, that it is our job to pause, give space, and that we are doing the best we can. Oliver's writing is very easy to read and speaks compassionately to counsellors and their clients. I really wish this book had been available to me in my fledgling years, as I really could have done with its encouragement and reassurance.

Mary Mackenzie

Couples Counsellor

REVIEWS

Ollie's book will become a bible for enthusiastic early career counsellors as well as experienced counsellors who may need some assistance to fan their enthusiasm in the, at times, complex world of couples counselling. It may even entice those counsellors who have run screaming from couples counselling vowing "never again". Ollie's down-to-earth approach, authenticity and gentle humour, helps to guide you to be the skilled umpire of the at times gruelling tennis match that can play out during a couples counselling session.

Ollie will help you with ideas to adeptly choreograph the intricate dance moves within the couple's relationship so there are less missteps or at the very least more laughter as they awkwardly at times step on each other's toes.

His years of counselling experience and knowledge shines a torch on strategies and tools which will help counsellors at any career stage navigate and make even more rewarding, the journey of couples counselling.

Lauren Cairnes

Registered Psychologist

As a fellow counsellor who works from an ACT and person-centred, trauma-informed lens, I found The Counsellor's Toolkit: Couples Counselling Through a Mental Health Lens both affirming and deeply practical. Ollie writes with a rare blend of clarity, compassion, and grounded humour, the kind that reminded me of why I chose this work in the first place.

Ollie's ability to transmute complex emotional and relational processes into human and hopeful language stands out most in this book. He captures the essence of couples' work, not as conflict management, but as nervous-system care and emotional repair. Every chapter feels like a conversation with a trusted colleague who invites you to slow down, stay curious, and meet clients where they are, rather than rushing to fix what's on the surface.

This book doesn't just offer techniques, it provides perspective. It honours the courage couples must show up and the vulnerability counsellors must hold that space authentically. It's full of insights, metaphors, and gentle reminders that healing happens in small, steady moments, the pause, the breath, the shared understanding that "it's never really about the dishwasher."

Whether you're new to the field or a seasoned practitioner, this book will leave you feeling grounded, inspired, and better equipped to support couples in finding their way back to safety and connection.

Adam Dear

Counsellor

INTRODUCTION

WHY THIS BOOK?

You've opened this book, which probably means one of two things. Either you're already in the trenches, trying to look wise and unflappable while two people argue about toothpaste with the intensity of a Supreme Court hearing; or you're about to start couples work and wondering whether you should memorise a few quotes from Rogers, practise your "thoughtful nod," and hope no one notices your heart thumping. Good news: you don't need to perform wisdom. You need to be human, curious, steady—and just brave enough to look beneath what's being said to what's really going on.

When I wrote my first book, I wanted to encourage new counsellors who felt they'd been handed a qualification and a chair and told, "Off you go—be helpful." In the second, I leaned into metaphors, because images reach places logic can't. This book is the next turn of the spiral. It's about couples, yes, but not in the "ten communication hacks and a date-night calendar" sense. It's about seeing couples work as mental health work. Not diagnosing and labelling, but recognising that every pause, every repair, every moment of validation is shaping a nervous system, quieting shame, and altering the course of a family.

Couples rarely arrive saying, "Hello, we're here because unresolved trauma and night-shift stress are kneading our marriage like pizza dough." They arrive with symptoms: the bins, the phone, the invisible scorecard about who cares more. The trap for us is to camp on the surface—refereeing the content—because content feels concrete. But if we only polish the dashboard light, the engine still burns oil. This book keeps pointing you under the bonnet.

A simple rule has served me in policing, in corporate life, and now in counselling: look for causes, not just symptoms. In the police, I learned how bodies carry stories: a jaw tightens, a knee bounces, a voice catches on one word. In the corporate world, I learned how systems can shape people's days so thoroughly that they forget what matters to them—then call their distress "performance issues." In counselling, those two worlds merge: the body tells us when it's not safe, the system around a couple (work, money, culture, family, history) tells us why it keeps not being safe. Our job is not to scold the symptoms. Our job is to help name the weather patterns.

Curiosity is how we do it. Not courtroom cross-examination; more like warm, persistent wondering. Curiosity is the counsellor's compass. It stops us from buying the first explanation. It lets us ask, "What do the dishes stand for? When did this feeling start? What does 'respect' look like to you in real life?" Curiosity softens judgement and invites story. Without it, we side with whichever partner is saying the words that sound most like our own. With it, we can sit inside two realities at once and say, "Both make sense." That stance alone reduces anxiety in the room. It also reduces our own: if my job is to be curious rather than to fix, I can breathe again.

I like to tell couples they have an invisible housemate. This housemate doesn't pay rent, never takes the bin out, and sleeps on the sofa of every conversation. Sometimes it's debt. Sometimes a new baby. Sometimes workplace "restructures" that happen so often they feel like a hobby. Sometimes it's trauma that's never had a name. The couple thinks they're fighting each other; they're really fighting the same housemate. When they see that, blame cools and teamwork warms. "It's not me versus you; it's us versus the load."

Here's a small story. A couple came to see me about time. She said he was always late: "He doesn't value me." He said she policed every minute: "I can't take a breath." With curiosity (and a lot of patience) we found her childhood lived under a father's rage—lateness meant danger. He grew up in chaos—time was a rumour and control was a threat. Add sleep debt, tight money, and two jobs. Punctuality wasn't the cause; it was the surface where older stories landed. When they saw that, the room softened. She wasn't crazy; she was scared. He wasn't careless; he was gasping. We still built some practical agreements about clocks, but now the agreements landed on compassion instead of concrete.

If we chase symptoms, two things happen. Couples get temporary relief and no real change, and we get tired—bone-tired—from refereeing matches we can't win. But when we step back, see the pattern, and ask cause-level questions, we stop firefighting and start weather-mapping. We notice the wind that keeps fanning sparks into flames. That's the difference between "talking it through" and healing.

Metaphors help. We'll use a few you'll see threaded through the chapters because they stick in people's minds. There's the garden weed: you can snip the leaves all day, but unless you pull the root—shame, fear, grief—it will be back by Tuesday. There's Newton's cradle: tit for tat, clackity clack, energy bouncing until someone chooses to still their ball. There's the pond: every word is a stone; the ripples reach children, workplaces, communities. There's the funhouse mirror: shame distorts, and people start to believe the distortion is truth. There's the hot potato: parents tossing anxiety to a child to cool their hands. And there's the speed bump: pausing isn't weakness; it's what saves the suspension.

If you've read my earlier work, you'll know humour lives here too. Not sarcasm, not superiority—just the lightness that lets truth land without shattering. When a couple is locked in the "socks-on-the-floor wars," a wry smile and "ah yes, the ancient conflict" can release enough air for curiosity to enter. Humour is physiological: it warms the nervous system, lowers the shoulders, lets breath come back. It's also ethical: it keeps us human.

The chapters that follow aren't lectures; they're conversations. We begin with the foundations: presence, empathy, congruence—Rogers' steady hand, not as a quote to recite but as a way to be. Without that ground, nothing grows. Then we move to observation and the art of seeing—really seeing—the micro-signals partners send and misread. We learn to ask better questions, not clever ones, and we learn to validate, because shame is the corrosive that eats trust from the inside. You'll hear a line you already know I love: "You seem to be doing the best you can." It's not indulgence. It's medicine for shame.

From there, we sit with reflection—not just the client's, ours as well. Reflection isn't a supervisory tick box; it's how authenticity grows. Without it, we become technicians. With it, we become humans who learn. Authenticity matters more than the perfect intervention. Couples smell performance; they relax with realness. Congruence isn't confession; it's clean presence. That leads to Chapter 7's quiet powerhouse: the pause. A beat of breath that changes the music.

Then compassion arrives—outward and inward. Compassion without differentiation becomes rescuing; differentiation without compassion becomes cold. Hold both and you get steadiness with warmth. We talk trust and safety as mental-health essentials, not romance extras. We explore conflict as a health issue, not a moral failure; we turn reactivity into regulation with rituals, repair attempts, and that humble speed bump. And when we widen the lens, the ripples become visible: how repaired conflict steadies kids; how safety travels in lunchboxes to workplaces; how cultures shift when dads apologise and mums stop carrying the whole emotional load.

We'll also talk about you. Self-care is not a scented add-on. It's what keeps your nervous system from leaking exhaustion into the room. Vicarious trauma is real. Compassion fatigue is real. Supervision is collective care, not administrative penance. Conversations with peers, gentle humour, boundaries you actually keep—these aren't indulgences. They are part of ethical practice because our presence is part of the intervention.

And then we gather the threads and say aloud the thing this book is really about: moving from symptoms to causes. Couples think they are fighting about toothpaste. Sometimes they are. Mostly they are fighting about safety, worth, control, belonging, grief. Our stance— authentic, curious, light—lets them look underneath without drowning. The metaphors help them remember how. And the mental-health lens gives the work its true heft: every pause is a trauma-informed act; every validation is shame-buffering; every repair is antidepressant in the wild.

A quick detour back to the invisible housemate. When you name it in the room, couples often look at each other like they have just caught the cat stealing chicken. There's relief in naming. "Oh. It's not that you don't care; it's that we're exhausted." "It's not that I'm impossible; it's that panic grabs my throat." Naming doesn't solve everything. It does change the tone. Tone is half the battle.

You'll also hear me repeat one little pivot that changes more arguments than any laminated worksheet: do what's helpful, say what's helpful. People rarely know what that is until you help them notice. "Stop being late" becomes "It helps me feel safe when you text if you're running behind." "Stop nagging" becomes "It helps me if we agree on two reminders and then let it be." The helpful/not helpful frame turns a fight into a shared plan.

Because we are talking about health, we'll keep naming the body. Anxiety, depression, trauma—they don't float above conversations like abstract clouds. They sit in the room, in tight jaws and shallow breaths, in eyes that dart away, in shoulders that rise when certain words are spoken. We'll keep treating conflict like second-hand smoke—it lingers in curtains and lungs long after the fight is over. And we'll keep teaching the pause and repair as the windows you open to let the air clear.

You'll meet triangulation properly when we get to the systemic chapters. Kids aren't just watching; they're recruited. Sometimes as peacekeepers. Sometimes as confessional boxes with school shoes on. The hot potato image sticks because families recognise it instantly: "We toss, the kid burns." It's not about blame; it's about awareness. Parents who can hold their own anxiety take the potato back. You can feel the relief in the child's body when they hear, "You don't have to fix us. That's our job."

Workplaces come into view too. The colleague who sits in a fog after another night of stonewalling; the nurse who copes because her partner says, "I'm with you"; the teacher who reaches kids because someone at home reaches her. Relationship health is workplace health. And culture gets a seat, because scripts matter. "Real men don't apologise." "A good wife swallows her feelings." These lines aren't quaint—they're health hazards.

Let's also be honest about our side of the glass. You will have clunky sessions. You'll over-explain one week and under-ask the next. You'll walk to your car replaying a sentence you wish you hadn't said. Reflection isn't for scolding; it's for calibrating. Humour isn't for deflection; it's for breathing. Supervision isn't for being graded;

it's for being human among humans who know what it costs to sit with pain. If you keep those three, you'll last—and more than last, you'll keep liking the work.

What won't you find here? Twenty-item checklists for "winning an argument in five steps." There's enough internet for that. You'll find stories, images, phrases, and questions that carry into the room the next day. You'll find reminders that your presence is an intervention and your steadiness is contagious. You'll find scripts to try—soft, human ones—like "Can we hold this for a second?" and "You seem to be doing the best you can," and "Same team." You'll also find permission to giggle when toothpaste turns into a metaphor for control and freedom, because sometimes that's exactly what it is.

A few quick road signs so you can feel the shape under your feet as you read. We begin with foundations: presence, empathy, congruence. Then we sharpen perception: observing patterns, asking questions that invite—not demand—truth, validating in ways that don't collapse into rescuing. We sit with reflection and authenticity so we don't turn into the cardboard counsellor who nods sagely while their soul checks email. We learn to pause. We practise compassion with boundaries—Bowen would call it differentiation. We build trust and safety as health infrastructure. We reframe conflict as something to regulate, not fear, and we play with rituals and repair so arguments don't own the week. We widen to ripples: kids, schools, teams, culture. We tend to ourselves as practitioners. And we close by gathering the metaphors and the stance—authentic, curious, lightly humorous—that let us keep choosing causes over symptoms when our own nerves are frayed.

If that sounds like a lot, that's because relationships contain multitudes. But you won't be doing it all at once. You'll be doing it one breath at a time, one pause, one "tell me more," one small repair that seems trivial until someone sleeps for the first time in months.

The big shapes of health are built out of tiny repeats. Couples don't become serene mystics; they become slightly steadier humans who can disagree without scaring each other half to death. That's victory.

Before we begin, a final word on tone. Counselling is ordinary and extraordinary at once. Ordinary, because we sit in quiet rooms and talk about bins and bedtimes and birthdays that went wrong. Extraordinary, because in those quiet rooms shame loosens its grip, people look at each other without armour for the first time in years, and the nervous system shifts from threat to safety. Hold both truths. They'll keep you grounded and grateful.

If you carry only one question from this introduction into your next session, make it this: "What's really going on here—beneath the surface?" Ask it kindly. Ask it often. Ask it of yourself when you feel pulled to fix or to prove. That question is the compass of this whole book. It points you from symptom to cause, from performance to presence, from cleverness to care.

And when the socks, toothpaste, or bins make their inevitable cameo, remember: they matter because life is lived in small things. But they're almost never just about the socks, toothpaste, or bins. They're about safety, worth, effort, grief, and hope clinking together in the cutlery basket. Breathe. Smile if you can. Ask a better question. Offer a clearer mirror. Drop a kinder stone in the pond. Help two bodies remember they can steady themselves and each other.

Ready? Let's begin.

CHAPTER 1

CURIOSITY & CORE CONDITIONS

I f you've been in a couples session for longer than ten minutes, chances are you've heard some version of this: *"He never loads the dishwasher properly."* Or, *"She always leaves her cups everywhere."* Or, *"We can't agree on who does what around the house."* On the surface, these are practical disagreements about chores. Domestic logistics. Who scrubs, who stacks, who folds. It's tempting to think that if they just agreed on a roster or divided the tasks fairly, the tension would disappear. But if you sit with enough couples, you soon realise it's rarely about the dishwasher.

The dishwasher is a decoy, a lightning rod. It's a place where deeper hurts find expression in a safe, containable way. It is easier to complain about cups left on the counter than to say, "I feel invisible in this relationship." It feels safer to argue about bins than to admit, "I don't feel like I matter to you." Couples bring their symptoms to counselling — the surface fights about dishes, laundry, or money — but what they are really carrying are symbols. The dishwasher stands in for fairness, respect, or appreciation. The pile of laundry becomes a proxy for whether one partner feels taken for granted. The forgotten shopping list becomes evidence in the case that one person doesn't listen or doesn't care.

When counsellors treat these arguments at face value, we fall into the trap of symptom management. We become referees with clipboards:

"Right, if you do dishes Monday and you do them Tuesday, and both promise to stop leaving mugs by the bed, you should be fine." But they won't be fine. Because the dishwasher was never about the dishwasher.

I once worked with a couple, names changed of course, James and Aisha. They'd been together twelve years and came into counselling because they "couldn't stop bickering." Their main battleground was the dishwasher. James loaded it "all wrong." Plates at odd angles, cups crammed in, cutlery scattered. Aisha would march in, sigh loudly, and reload it her way. James accused her of being controlling. She accused him of being careless. Round and round they went until the dishwasher became the enemy.

Now, I could have suggested a rota or referred them to a financial advisor if their fights had been about money. But I'm not in the business of surface fixes. Instead, I invited them to slow down and asked: *"What does the dishwasher mean to each of you?"* At first, they looked at me as if I had lost the plot. But curiosity has a way of opening doors. As we peeled back the layers, their stories emerged. For Aisha, order was safety. She'd grown up in a chaotic household where nothing was predictable. Structure was her lifeline. A messy dishwasher wasn't just untidy — it triggered an old fear of chaos creeping back in. For James, being criticised over the dishwasher felt like rejection. He had grown up with constant criticism, carrying the message that he was never good enough. Every sigh, every reloaded plate reinforced that wound.

The problem was not the dishwasher. The problem was the deeper meaning each had attached to it, shaped by history, stress, and unspoken fears. Once they could see that, the conversation shifted. Suddenly they weren't fighting about plates. They were talking about safety, belonging, and worth. That shift is a mental health intervention. By reframing symptoms as symbols, the couple could understand their reactivity not as personal flaws but as nervous system responses rooted in past pain.

When we, as counsellors, approach these dynamics with curiosity, we are doing more than solving problems. We are supporting mental health. Aisha's anxiety calmed when her fear of chaos was named. James' shame softened when his wound of never being good enough was recognised. Their arguments began to make sense to them, and that in itself was regulating. The nervous system loves meaning.

This is why I hold on tightly to the principle of helpful versus not helpful. Aisha saying, *"You never load the dishwasher properly"* is not helpful. It shames. James saying, *"You're always criticising me"* is not helpful. It accuses. But reframing those statements makes a difference. Aisha could instead say, *"It helps me feel calmer when the plates are stacked neatly."* James could say, *"It helps me feel appreciated when you notice the times I get it right."* These are still complaints, but they are transformed into requests. They create collaboration rather than attack. Couples who practise this shift begin to notice changes not just in their relationship but in their mental health. Anxiety reduces because they are speaking constructively. Shame lifts because they are being heard without blame.

As counsellors, we can model this in the room. When one partner launches into criticism, I sometimes pause and ask, *"What would be helpful for you instead?"* That single question can pivot the whole session. It moves the couple from symptom management to cause exploration. It grounds them in curiosity rather than reactivity.

Pausing itself is a powerful intervention. Couples in reactive cycles rarely stop to breathe. The dishwasher loads, the sigh comes, the retort fires back, all before anyone has had a chance to reflect. A pause interrupts this rhythm. It makes space for curiosity to enter. Sometimes I'll literally hold up my hand and say, *"Let's pause. What just happened there?"* Or I'll invite one partner to repeat what they just said, but slower. The nervous system calms in that gap, and meaning has a chance to emerge.

I often use the metaphor of the iceberg to help couples understand this. The dishwasher, the bins, the shopping list — these are the tip of the iceberg, the part above the waterline. But beneath the surface lies the bulk: the histories, the stresses, the attachment wounds, the unspoken needs. That's where the real work lies. If we spend all our time chipping away at the visible tip, nothing changes. But if we dive into the depths, couples begin to see the causes that drive their symptoms.

For many, this reframing is the first time they've considered that their fights are not about what they think they are about. It is also the first time they see their own nervous system at play. Trauma responses, shame cycles, and anxiety triggers are not flaws; they are survival strategies. Recognising that can reduce self-blame and build compassion. Instead of saying, *"You're just lazy"* or *"You're controlling"*, they can begin to say, *"This is how my nervous system reacts when I feel unsafe"*. That shift is enormous. It is the difference between blame and understanding, between escalation and regulation.

The work begins with curiosity, but it takes shape through the questions we ask. A well-placed question — *"What does this mean for you?"* — becomes a bridge. It leads from symptoms to causes, from conflict to compassion. The mental health of both partners improves not because their dishwasher is suddenly loaded the "right" way, but because they begin to see and soothe each other's hidden wounds.

This is why I often remind myself that when a couple is bickering about chores, they're not really asking me to referee. They are asking me to help them find each other again beneath the noise. My job isn't to fix the dishwasher. It's to help them uncover what the dishwasher symbolises and, in doing so, to create space for healing.

Couples rarely come into the room to talk about their childhood traumas. They come to talk about lateness, money, phones, in-laws, sex, or the "right" way to fold towels. The surface issues change from couple to couple, but the pattern is the same. These arguments are rarely about what they appear to be. They are doorways into something much bigger. Curiosity at the start of the first session leads me to ask questions about everyone's childhood. What was school like? Can you tell me about your parents and your siblings in your childhood and now? What were extra-curricular activities like? Did you have a dog or a cat? Do you have a dog or a cat? What are your hobbies now? When I hear symptoms like the dishwasher, I am better positioned to understand where the cause originated.

Emma and Michael were a good example. Their battleground wasn't dishes but punctuality. Emma grew tense if they weren't in the car ten minutes early. Michael moved at his own pace, unbothered if they left a few minutes late. In session, Emma accused Michael of disrespecting her. He accused her of being controlling. At first glance, I could have tried to negotiate a middle ground: she eases off a little, he hurries up a little. That compromise might have reduced friction for a week or two, but it wouldn't have solved anything.

Curiosity pushed us further. I asked Emma, "What happens for you inside when you think you might be late?" She paused, then admitted, "My chest tightens. I hear my father yelling again. He hated lateness, and if we weren't ready on time, he'd shout until the house shook." For Emma, punctuality wasn't about respect for schedules — it was about safety. Her nervous system had learned to equate lateness with danger.

I turned to Michael. "And when Emma insists on leaving early, what does that mean for you?" He leaned back. "It feels like being trapped. Growing up, there were no rules, no consistency. Everyone did their own thing. I learned to value freedom, not the clock. When she pushes me, I feel like I'm being controlled."

Suddenly, their fights weren't about minutes on a clock. They were about trauma and identity. Emma's anxiety was ignited by memories of fear. Michael's need for autonomy was born of chaos. Their arguments had been mislabelled for years. When they began to see the roots, their mental health benefitted. Emma realised her panic wasn't irrational — it was a conditioned response. Michael realised his resistance wasn't laziness — it was protection. Naming these causes helped them both find compassion, and compassion is medicine for the nervous system.

Money is another common flashpoint. Sarah and Luke argued endlessly about spending. She accused him of being tight-fisted. He accused her of being reckless. If I had tried to referee, I would have been out of my depth. I'm not a financial planner, and even if I were, a budget wouldn't have addressed what was really going on. So I asked them each to share what money meant to them.

Sarah said, "Money means freedom. I grew up with nothing. We could never afford anything. Spending now means I've escaped all that. It feels like joy, like proof that I survived."

Luke's face was tight as he replied, "For me, money means security. My parents split up, and I can still see Mum crying over bills. Saving is the only way I know how to feel safe. Watching money go out makes me feel like everything might collapse again."

It wasn't pounds and pence they were arguing over. It was freedom and security, joy and fear, scarcity and safety. Once those meanings surfaced, the sting began to ease. Sarah stopped labelling Luke a miser. Luke stopped labelling Sarah reckless. They began to see what each of them was trying to protect. By naming the underlying causes, their fights stopped being personal attacks and started being joint battles against stress.

Then there was Tom and Priya, who came in saying they had a "sex problem." They hadn't been intimate in a year. Tom felt rejected. Priya felt pressured. The conversation could have stayed stuck on frequency and technique, but that would have missed the point. As Priya talked, it became clear she was carrying an enormous load: full-time work, managing the household, and caring for her chronically ill mother. She wasn't uninterested in Tom; she was exhausted. Tom, meanwhile, wasn't just chasing sex for physical reasons. For him, intimacy was his main way of feeling connected. Without it, he spiralled into doubt and shame.

Here again, the fight wasn't about sex. It was about psychosocial stress crushing Priya's capacity, and about Tom's deep need for reassurance. Once the stress was acknowledged, they could stop blaming each other. They began to ask different questions: "How can we share the load differently?" "How can we create space for rest and play?" With less weight on Priya, intimacy returned naturally. The mental health link was clear: stress management opened the door to connection.

In each of these cases — lateness, money, intimacy — the surface argument disguised a deeper story. I often tell couples, "It looks like you're fighting each other, but really you're both fighting stress. It just wears a different disguise for each of you." That simple reframing externalises the problem. It's not Emma versus Michael, or Sarah versus Luke, or Tom versus Priya. It's trauma, anxiety, scarcity, exhaustion. When the enemy shifts from partner to stress, the couple moves from adversaries to allies.

The implications for mental health are profound. Anxiety no longer needs to be hidden in defensiveness. Shame no longer needs to harden into blame. Depression no longer has to sit in silence. When couples externalise their struggles and see stress as the opponent, their nervous systems calm. They move out of survival mode and into collaboration.

For counsellors, the key is not to get trapped in the weeds of the symptom. It's tempting to jump into problem-solving: a rota for chores, a budget for spending, a schedule for sex. These might patch things temporarily, but they do little for long-term wellbeing. What matters is the meaning beneath. Our questions need to uncover what the symptom represents.

Sometimes the work is as simple as reframing. Instead of "He's late because he doesn't care," it becomes "He's late because punctuality doesn't trigger the same alarms in him that it does in me." Instead of "She spends because she's careless," it becomes "She spends because she's trying to reclaim joy after years of scarcity." Instead of "He doesn't want sex because he doesn't love me," it becomes "He's drowning in exhaustion, not rejection." These reframings do not excuse behaviour, but they contextualise it. Context reduces shame. Context fosters empathy. Context supports mental health.

I often describe stress as a fog. When you're in it, everything looks distorted. You bump into each other, misinterpret movements, stumble over things you would normally navigate with ease. Couples in conflict often live in this fog. They see only blurred outlines of each other, and every collision feels intentional. The counsellor's role is not to clear the fog completely — life stressors can't be erased — but to shine enough light for couples to see what's really happening. Once they can see each other more clearly, they stop blaming and start collaborating.

The lesson is the same across all the examples: surface fights are never just surface fights. They are doorways to histories, identities, fears, and longings. They are symptoms pointing to causes. When couples learn to look beneath the dishwasher, beneath the lateness, beneath the spending, they begin to understand themselves and each other in ways that support not just their relationship but their mental health.

If there is one dynamic that undoes couples more than any other, it is reactivity. A comment is made, a sigh escapes, a door closes a little harder than usual, and suddenly the room is filled with tension. Arguments that begin with something small escalate into something much bigger. What started as a question about whether the bin was taken out becomes a battle of raised voices, icy silences, or tears. The speed with which things can unravel is often breathtaking.

This is not about couples being inherently bad at communication. It is about the nervous system doing its job. When people feel threatened — not just physically, but emotionally — their bodies react. One partner may go into fight mode, their voice rising, their words sharpening. Another may withdraw into flight or freeze, shutting down to escape intensity. Sometimes a partner fawns, appeasing quickly to avoid conflict. None of these are conscious choices. They are survival strategies, learned long before the current relationship, often rooted in trauma, anxiety, or family-of-origin patterns. But when both partners' survival systems are activated at once, the cycle can feel relentless.

Sam and Leanne illustrate this well. Whenever conflict began, Sam withdrew. His arms crossed, his gaze dropped, his voice disappeared. Leanne, feeling shut out, escalated. She raised her voice, followed him from room to room, demanding answers. The more she pursued, the more he retreated. The more he retreated, the louder she became. She called him a stone wall. He called her a nag. Both felt hopeless.

But when we slowed things down and invited curiosity, a different picture emerged. For Sam, withdrawing was a freeze response. He had grown up in a home where conflict could turn violent. Silence and retreat had once been his safest option. For Leanne, raised in a family where everything was aired loudly and immediately, his withdrawal felt like abandonment. It triggered her fear of being left, so she pursued harder. Neither was trying to hurt the other. Both were trying to survive.

I sometimes use the metaphor of a tennis match to help couples see this. Imagine the argument as a rally. Sam withdraws — the serve. Leanne raises her voice — the return. Sam retreats further — the backhand slice. Leanne pursues harder — the smash. Back and forth it goes until both are exhausted. The problem isn't Sam or Leanne. The problem is the game they are caught in. When couples can see their arguments as a rally rather than a moral failing, they begin to externalise the problem. Instead of saying, "You always run away" or "You never stop yelling," they can begin to say, "We've both been dragged into the rally." The cycle itself becomes the opponent.

This shift is not just intellectual. It has deep mental health implications. When couples see reactivity as a nervous system response, not a character flaw, shame reduces. Shame is one of the most corrosive forces in relationships. It fuels depression, feeds anxiety, and leaves people feeling unworthy. To reframe a partner's shouting as fear rather than aggression, or withdrawal as protection rather than laziness, can be profoundly healing. It allows compassion to grow in the very places where contempt once flourished.

The pause is one of the most effective ways to break this rally. Like a time-out in sport, the pause interrupts momentum. In session, I often hold up a hand and say, "Let's pause. What just happened there?" It slows the room down enough for each partner to reflect rather than react. In one pause, Sam was able to say, "When you raise your voice,

I feel unsafe. My body shuts down." Leanne was able to respond, "When you go quiet, I panic. I feel like you're leaving me." For the first time, they were explaining instead of accusing. That shift turned a tennis rally into a conversation.

Curiosity also serves as a pattern-breaker. Instead of assuming what their partner's behaviour means, I encourage couples to ask. "When you went quiet just now, what was happening for you?" "When you raised your voice, what were you hoping I'd hear?" These questions are not easy to ask in the heat of conflict, but with practice, they transform reactivity into understanding. Behaviour is no longer misinterpreted as malice but seen as a signal.

This is also where the principle of helpful versus not helpful is invaluable. In the midst of reactivity, partners often focus on what they don't want: "Don't shut me out." "Stop yelling." These statements, while understandable, usually escalate tension. Reframing them into helpful requests changes everything. Leanne learned to say, "It helps me when you tell me you need space but that you'll come back." Sam learned to say, "It helps me when you lower your voice — I can hear you better then." These are small linguistic shifts, but they move the couple from criticism to collaboration, from shame to safety.

When couples begin to practise this, their mental health improves noticeably. Anxiety decreases because they no longer sit in cycles of catastrophic interpretation. Depression lightens because they feel heard and validated. Trauma responses soften because the nervous system learns that the present is not the past. Helpful language is more than good communication — it is emotional regulation in action.

For counsellors, the challenge is to stay grounded when reactivity fills the room. Couples can pull us into their rallies, leaving us flustered or drained. I often ask myself: "Am I noticing my own nervous system tightening? Am I tempted to fire off interventions like a novice salesperson throwing products at a prospect?" When I catch myself in that mode, I slow down. I return to curiosity. I remind myself that my job is not to break the rally by force but to invite the couple to see it differently.

I also remind myself of the fire alarm metaphor. Reactivity is like a smoke alarm — loud, urgent, impossible to ignore. But alarms don't always mean there's a fire. Sometimes it's just burnt toast. In relationships, a raised voice or a slammed door is the alarm. The instinct is to react immediately — shout back, chase, retreat further. But if we pause, we can ask, "What is setting off this alarm?" Maybe it's fear. Maybe it's shame. Maybe it's sheer exhaustion. Helping couples see reactivity as an alarm rather than an attack makes space for empathy.

The work of breaking reactivity is not about eliminating conflict. It's about teaching couples to handle conflict without destroying connection. The nervous system will still flare, but when couples can pause, ask, and reframe, they begin to regulate each other rather than dysregulate. Over time, the tennis rallies shorten. The alarms quieten. The fog lifts just enough for partners to see each other again.

For me, this is one of the most rewarding parts of the work. To watch a couple move from "You're impossible" to "I get scared when you do that" is to witness healing in real time. It's not flashy. It doesn't make for dramatic television. But it restores dignity, and dignity is the bedrock of mental health.

By the time couples arrive at counselling, they've usually tried everything they can think of to solve their conflicts. They've negotiated rotas, promised to do better, read the self-help blogs, maybe even bought the "his and hers" chore charts. Yet here they are, still at war over bins, money, or intimacy. When we as counsellors sit across from them, there's a temptation to think our role is to finally deliver the perfect tool or technique — the thing that will make it all work. But more often than not, what shifts the ground beneath them isn't a clever exercise or worksheet. It's the quality of the relationship in the room.

This is where Carl Rogers' core conditions become more than lofty ideals. Empathy, congruence, and unconditional positive regard are not abstract theories — they are practical foundations. Couples rarely say it out loud, but what they long for most is empathy: to have the pain beneath their complaint heard. They long for congruence: to meet a counsellor who shows up as a real human being rather than a detached referee with a clipboard. They long for unconditional positive regard: to know that even in their messiest, most reactive moments, they are still worthy of care and respect.

When I remind myself of this, I feel a kind of relief. I don't need to have the perfect intervention ready. I need to be present. A well-timed moment of empathy — "I can hear how much this hurts" — can be more regulating for a couple's nervous systems than any elaborate strategy. A genuine laugh at the absurdity of human relationships can soften shame more effectively than a carefully crafted diagram. A steady, calm presence in the heat of conflict can do more to anchor a couple than a library of theories.

The irony is that counsellors, especially newer ones, often forget this. We sit in sessions worrying about whether we're doing it "right." Should I be asking more open questions? Should I be leaning into CBT? Should I introduce a systemic frame? In those moments, we're no longer with the couple. We've stepped into our own heads, tangled in self-doubt. We're what I call "out of our minds" — not in the sense of losing it completely, but of losing presence.

Back to the novice salesperson. Instead of listening to what the customer actually needs, the rookie panics and throws every product in the catalogue at them: "Here's a warranty, here's an add-on, here's a premium upgrade." The customer, overwhelmed, disengages. They can't see the value because they can't connect it to their real requirements. We can be the same in the therapy room. When anxiety gets the better of us, we hurl metaphors, theories, and interventions like confetti. We hope something sticks, but the couple is left dazed. They don't need the whole catalogue. They need presence. They need us to slow down, to listen, to connect what we're offering to the beating heart of their lived experience.

I remember a peer telling me how she once panicked in session and tried to deliver everything she had learned in training in the space of one hour. Every skill, every intervention, every reflective question. The couple left confused, she left exhausted, and nothing much changed. What they needed was not the entire syllabus. They needed her presence, her curiosity, and her willingness to believe that beneath the conflict there was something human worth uncovering.

When we, as counsellors, learn to resist the panic of over-offering, we become more effective. We trust that our role is not to fix the dishwasher, the lateness, or the spending. It is to help couples name what those arguments symbolise. And often, that alone is enough. The moment a couple sees their fight about money as a fight about freedom and safety, the air shifts. The moment they recognise that reactivity is not malice but a nervous system response, they soften. The moment they speak in helpful language instead of unhelpful blame, they create a path back to connection.

These are not just communication tweaks. They are mental health interventions. Anxiety, depression, and trauma responses thrive in blame, shame, and chaos. They ease in empathy, curiosity, and regulation. The tools we use — reframing, pausing, helpful language

— all serve one purpose: to create space where partners can regulate each other rather than dysregulate. And that, more than any rota or budget, is what sustains relationships.

As I sit with these reflections, I often ask myself: when have I been "out of my mind" in a session? When have I been more concerned with my performance than with the couple in front of me? What helped me return to presence? Sometimes it's noticing my own breath. Sometimes it's catching the humour in the situation. Sometimes it's remembering Rogers' conditions: empathy, congruence, unconditional positive regard. These are my anchors. They pull me back into the room, back into curiosity, back into what really matters.

Couples will continue to fight about dishwashers, lateness, money, sex, and towels. That is inevitable. But beneath those symptoms lie causes waiting to be uncovered: histories of chaos, scars of criticism, legacies of scarcity, layers of stress. Our task is not to tidy up the symptoms. Our task is to guide couples toward the causes. To create the conditions where those causes can be spoken aloud without fear. To remind them that even in the fog, even in the tennis rallies, even in the clatter of cutlery and crockery, they are not enemies. They are two people longing to feel safe, valued, and connected.

And if all else fails, sometimes the most powerful thing we can do is smile, hold the space, and remember: it's never really about the dishwasher.

CHAPTER 2

OBSERVATION & CURIOSITY

One of the most underrated skills in counselling is observation. Not observation in the sense of sitting back with a clipboard and ticking off behaviours, but the kind of deep noticing that tunes into what is being said and, just as importantly, what is not being said. Couples bring us their words, but their bodies often tell the real story. A clenched jaw, a tapping foot, an averted gaze — these are signals just as powerful as any sentence. They are windows into stress, shame, fear, and longing. And for many clients, those signals are the unspoken cry for help.

My own background in policing sharpened this instinct. In interviews with suspects or witnesses, words were often the least reliable evidence. People lied, misremembered, or told the story in a way that protected them. But bodies betrayed the truth: the glance at the door, the twitch in the hand, the sudden stillness in a room full of noise. Observation was survival. It helped me sense danger, dishonesty, or distress before words caught up.

When I transitioned into counselling, I realised how transferable this skill was. Only now the goal was not to catch someone out, but to tune into where their pain was hiding. Couples, like suspects in an interview, sometimes present a polished story. They come in insisting the problem is about dishes or phones, but their bodies tell a deeper tale. The partner who insists they are "fine" might sit hunched over, arms wrapped tightly around themselves, betraying the anxiety beneath. The partner who swears they're "done trying" might lean forward unconsciously, showing they still long for connection.

Observation allows us to notice these things and bring them into the room. It is not about accusing or confronting but about curiosity. "I notice your voice got quieter when you said that — what was happening for you then?" or "When you talk about money, I see you glance away from your partner — what's that like for you?" These questions open doors. They invite clients to notice their own inner experience, which often gets buried beneath automatic reactions.

Observation is more than noticing discomfort. It's also about catching the moments of lightness that clients often overlook. The softening of the eyes when a partner recalls a happy memory. The small smile when they admit, "Actually, I did miss you." These glimmers are vital. They remind couples that their relationship is not only defined by stress. From a mental health perspective, they anchor clients in hope. Anxiety and depression can shrink people's vision until they see only conflict. By pointing out the micro-moments of warmth, we help them reclaim balance.

Curiosity is the companion to observation. Without curiosity, observation risks turning into judgement. With curiosity, observation becomes a bridge. I once worked with a couple, Harry and Tori, who came in complaining about constant sniping. Harry accused Tori of being critical. Tori accused Harry of being detached. During the session, I noticed something small: whenever Harry spoke, Tori would cross her arms and lean back slightly. I said gently, "Tori, I notice your arms fold whenever Harry is speaking. What's happening for you when that happens?" She sighed, "I don't even realise I'm doing it. I suppose it's my way of bracing for more disappointment."

That moment shifted the energy in the room. Harry stopped defending and started listening. Tori stopped blaming and began reflecting. What could have been dismissed as a body tic became an entry point to her vulnerability. Her defensive posture was not malice but protection. Harry saw that, and the sting of criticism softened. The power of observation lay not in me spotting the arms crossing but in me holding it with curiosity.

This has direct relevance to mental health. Many of our clients arrive carrying layers of stress and trauma. Their nervous systems are often in overdrive, stuck in fight, flight, freeze, or fawn. These states show up in their bodies long before they show up in their words. A jittering leg can reveal anxiety. A slumped posture can speak of depression. A fixed smile can mask grief. Observation helps us name what the body already knows, which in turn helps the client connect the dots. For couples, this is especially important. Partners often misread each other's signals. One sees withdrawal and interprets rejection. The other sees raised voices and interprets attack. If we can pause and name what is happening beneath the surface, we help couples reframe these signals. Withdrawal becomes "I'm scared." Anger becomes "I'm desperate for connection." The mental health benefits are obvious: shame reduces, fear softens, compassion grows.

This is where Rogers' core conditions echo again. Empathy is not only about listening to words — it is about attuning to the whole person. Congruence means that if I notice something in the room, I share it honestly but kindly, not hiding behind silence. Unconditional positive regard means I treat even defensive or hostile behaviours as survival strategies rather than flaws. Observation helps us live these conditions in practice. It grounds empathy in the body, not just the intellect.

Curiosity deepens the process further. Curiosity is not interrogation. It is not cross-examination. It is an attitude, a posture of wondering.

"What's really happening here?" "What does this mean for you?" "What story does this connect to?" Curiosity keeps us from rushing to solutions. It reminds us that behaviour is always communication, even when the words don't line up.

I often tell clients that curiosity is the antidote to reactivity. Reactivity assumes. It leaps to conclusions: "You're ignoring me." "You're attacking me." Curiosity pauses and asks: "What's going on inside you right now?" When couples practise this, their mental health benefits. Anxiety decreases because they no longer catastrophise every silence. Depression lightens because they feel seen rather than judged. Relationships stabilise because partners learn to interpret signals more accurately.

One of the simplest but most powerful techniques I use is mirroring. Not in the sense of copying body language, but in the sense of reflecting back what I've observed. "I noticed you looked down when you said that." "I hear you describing yourself as lazy, but I see someone carrying an enormous load." These reflections often move clients to tears — or at least to honesty. They help people feel recognised not just in their words but in their whole selves. That recognition is a mental health intervention in itself. When someone feels fully seen, shame loosens its grip.

Of course, observation and curiosity can be mishandled. Used carelessly, they can feel intrusive. If I pounce on every twitch or sigh, clients will feel scrutinised, not supported. The art lies in timing and tone. I try to make my curiosity invitational rather than forensic. "Would it be okay if I shared something I noticed?" "Can I check in with you about the way you just looked away?" This way, clients feel respected rather than exposed. Respect is not just a courtesy — it is the foundation of safety, and safety is what allows trauma to surface without retraumatising.

Observation also helps us notice the couple's interaction as a whole. Sometimes the most telling thing is not what either partner does individually, but how they move in relation to each other. Do they talk over each other constantly? Do they wait carefully for turns? Do they mirror each other's posture without realising it? These small dynamics reveal volumes about the health of the relationship. Couples who interrupt compulsively may be fighting for space. Couples who sit in synchrony may be more connected than they realise. Pointing this out gently can help them see their own dance more clearly.

When I think about observation and curiosity in the counselling room, I often come back to the image of a detective — but not the detective who barges in demanding confessions. More like the detective who quietly gathers clues, pieces together the story, and helps others see what was invisible before. Our job is not to solve the mystery for couples but to help them uncover the meaning behind their own behaviours. And in doing so, we support not only their relationship but their mental health.

Observation opens the door, but it is curiosity and validation that help clients walk through it. Couples can endure years of misinterpretation because no one has ever paused long enough to ask what lies beneath a behaviour, and no one has ever offered validation when the answer finally comes. Without validation, even the best observations and questions can land flat. A partner might reveal a painful truth only to feel dismissed or minimised. That absence of validation is not just discouraging; it can deepen wounds and worsen mental health outcomes.

I often describe validation as the emotional equivalent of oxygen. Without it, conversations suffocate. With it, they breathe. Validation doesn't mean agreeing with everything a partner says. It doesn't mean endorsing harmful behaviour. It simply means acknowledging that the emotion makes sense in the context of their lived experience. When Emma says, "I panic when we're late because my father used to yell at me," validation sounds like, "That makes sense. Anyone who grew up with that kind of fear would probably feel the same." When Michael says, "I feel trapped when you insist on timing everything," validation is, "Of course that would matter to you if freedom has always been your way of coping."

These moments matter more than most people realise. Many clients come into counselling with deep histories of invalidation. They've been told, "You're too sensitive," "You're overreacting," "Just get over it," and the classic, "You're over thinking." Over time, these messages chip away at self-worth and feed anxiety and depression. To have their emotions finally validated in the therapy room is profoundly healing. It doesn't fix everything, but it creates a platform of safety on which new patterns can be built.

Curiosity is what gets us there. Genuine curiosity is not a trick; it is a posture of respect. It says, "I don't assume I know you — I want to understand." For many couples, this is a revelation. They have spent years assuming: "He leaves late because he doesn't care," "She nags because she enjoys it." When they learn to replace assumption with curiosity, something shifts. The conversation moves from accusation to exploration, from reactivity to reflection.

I recall a session with a couple, Julia and Ben. Julia was furious that Ben spent hours gaming in the evenings. She felt abandoned and unwanted. Ben felt attacked for the one hobby that helped him switch off. At first, the conversation was the usual round of blame. But curiosity nudged us into deeper territory. I asked Ben, "What does gaming give you that nothing else does?" He hesitated, then said, "It's the only time my head goes quiet. I've had panic attacks since I was a teenager. Gaming distracts me long enough that I don't feel like I'm drowning."

Julia's face softened immediately. For years, she thought he was choosing the console over her. She never knew it was his way of managing anxiety. Suddenly, the problem wasn't "Ben is selfish." The problem was "Ben is trying to cope with a mental health struggle in a way that leaves Julia lonely." That shift didn't erase the tension, but it reframed it in a way that created compassion. Julia could validate his need for calm. Ben could validate her need for connection. From there, they could explore alternatives together.

Validation also protects against escalation. When partners feel unheard, they repeat themselves louder and louder, desperate for recognition. Once they feel validated, the nervous system calms. Cortisol drops, breathing slows, empathy becomes possible again. From a mental health perspective, validation is regulation. It helps partners step out of survival mode and back into their prefrontal cortex where problem-solving lives.

Curiosity is powerful, but like any tool, it can be misused. Too many questions, especially fired off quickly, can feel like interrogation. I learned this the hard way early in my practice. I thought being curious meant asking lots of questions, one after another, digging and digging until I struck gold. Instead, I often struck resistance. Clients would shut down, feel scrutinised, or accuse me of picking them apart. I came to understand that curiosity without pacing can overwhelm. This is where the principle of "less is best" begins to show its importance.

Curiosity is most effective when it is spacious. It is less about how many questions we ask and more about which ones. A single, well-timed question can open a conversation for an hour. "What does this mean for you?" can go further than ten rapid-fire probes. Curiosity needs room to breathe. It needs silence to follow it. Couples often need time to reflect before they can articulate what lies beneath their patterns. When we fill that silence with more questions, we can inadvertently shut down the very insights we are trying to invite.

This is where observation, curiosity, and validation weave together. Observation gives us the clues. Curiosity opens the door. Validation makes it safe to step through. Without observation, our curiosity might miss the point. Without curiosity, our observations remain assumptions. Without validation, our curiosity feels hollow. When all three work together, the counselling room becomes a space where clients can see themselves and each other more clearly than ever before.

The mental health implications here are enormous. Couples who practise curiosity and validation in their daily lives build resilience against stress. Instead of spiralling into catastrophic assumptions, they pause and ask. Instead of shutting each other down with criticism, they validate. These habits protect against the erosion of self-worth, reduce anxiety, and foster a sense of safety. Safety is the soil where intimacy grows. Without it, relationships starve. With it, they flourish.

I often find myself circling back to Rogers in this context. His belief that empathy, congruence, and unconditional positive regard are not luxuries but necessities resonates deeply here. Validation is empathy in action. Curiosity is congruence in practice — showing up authentically, willing to admit we don't know and eager to learn. And unconditional positive regard underpins it all. To sit with a couple in their most raw and reactive moments and still see them as worthy is to create the very conditions that make healing possible.

Sometimes I use metaphors to make this accessible to clients. I tell them curiosity is like a torch in a dark room. Without it, they stumble around, tripping over the same obstacles again and again. With it, they can finally see where they're going. Validation is like water on dry soil. Without it, seeds of change wither. With it, those seeds have a chance to grow. Observation is the map that shows them where they are. Each one is vital, but together they create movement, growth, and hope.

I also remind couples that these skills are not just "for the relationship." They are mental health practices in their own right. People who live with anxiety benefit when their partners approach them with curiosity instead of judgement. People who live with depression find relief when their feelings are validated instead of dismissed. People carrying trauma feel safer when their non-verbal signals are noticed and respected. In that sense, observation, curiosity, and validation are not just relational tools; they are acts of care that sustain psychological wellbeing.

Curiosity is one of our most powerful tools as counsellors, but like any tool, it can cause harm if used carelessly. Questions can open doors, but they can also shut them just as quickly. This is where the art comes in — knowing not only what to ask, but when to stop asking.

I sometimes think of questions as scalpels. In the right hands, a scalpel can save a life. In the wrong hands, or used too frequently, it can do damage. Counsellors who fire off too many questions in quick succession often leave clients feeling dissected rather than understood. For couples already carrying anxiety or depression, that sense of being under the microscope can increase stress. Instead of feeling safe, they feel scrutinised. Instead of feeling validated, they feel as though they are failing some unseen test.

This is why the principle of "less is best" matters so much. A single well-placed question, followed by silence, can be far more powerful than a flurry of inquiries. Silence is not emptiness — it is space. It allows clients' nervous systems to settle and their stories to emerge.

When we rush to fill the silence with more questions, we often interrupt the very insight that was about to surface.

I remember a couple, Hannah and Leo, who came in after months of bitter conflict. In the first session, I was eager to get to the root of things. I peppered them with questions: "How long has this been happening?" "What happens next?" "What did you feel when that happened?" By the end of the session, they looked more exhausted than when they arrived. I had mistaken interrogation for curiosity.

In the second session, I slowed down. I asked one question — "What hurts most about this for you?" — and then I waited. It felt like an eternity in the silence that followed. But then Hannah's eyes filled with tears and she said, "I feel like I'm invisible in his world." That one line told me more than a dozen questions ever could. Leo shifted in his chair and said quietly, "I had no idea you felt that way. I thought you just hated me." The entire session turned on that moment. Less had been more.

From a mental health perspective, restraint protects clients from overwhelm. Anxiety thrives when people feel interrogated. Depression deepens when people feel misunderstood or unheard. Trauma survivors, in particular, can be retraumatised by rapid-fire questioning that mirrors the intensity of past interrogations or confrontations. By slowing down, we regulate the pace of the session. We show that exploration can happen without force, that safety and patience are part of the process.

Another pitfall of questioning is the subtle pressure it places on clients to perform. Couples sometimes come in expecting to be graded, like students in a classroom. Every question feels like a test with a right or wrong answer. When counsellors over-question, we inadvertently reinforce this anxiety. Clients start giving us what they think we want to hear rather than what is true for them. The result is surface compliance without deeper change.

One of the ways I try to counter this is by replacing some questions with reflections or invitations. Instead of asking, "Why did you react that way?" I might say, "I notice your face tightened when you said that. I wonder what was happening inside for you." Instead of asking, "Do you think you could have handled that differently?" I might offer, "That sounded painful. What would have felt more helpful for you in that moment?" These invitations are still curious, but they feel less like a spotlight and more like an open door.

The distinction between mirroring and paraphrasing is also helpful here. Mirroring is reflecting back the exact words the client used, like holding up a mirror so they can see themselves clearly. Paraphrasing involves putting their words into our own. Both can be useful, but mirroring in particular allows clients to hear their own words afresh, without distortion. Sometimes this alone creates the pause they need to reflect. And because it's not another question, it avoids the sense of interrogation.

"Less is best" also matters because couples often interrogate each other outside the therapy room. "Why are you always like this?" "What's wrong with you?" "Why can't you just...?" These questions fuel shame, not insight. If we replicate that pattern in the counselling room, even unintentionally, we reinforce the cycle. By modelling spaciousness, we offer an alternative. We show that understanding can emerge from curiosity rather than interrogation, and that healing conversations often have more silence than words.

There is also the issue of counsellor anxiety. When we feel unsure of what to do next, our default can be to ask another question. It feels active, like we're moving things along. But often this is about soothing our own discomfort rather than serving the client. Rogers warned of this when he emphasised congruence. If I'm firing off questions because I'm nervous, I'm not being congruent. I'm hiding my anxiety behind a wall of curiosity. Clients sense this, and it erodes trust. Sometimes the most congruent thing to do is simply acknowledge what is happening: "I notice I'm feeling a bit stuck. Can we sit with that together?" That honesty itself can be grounding for clients.

The mental health implications are clear. Clients who experience gentle curiosity instead of interrogation feel safer. Safety is the foundation for trauma healing, the antidote to anxiety, and the anchor for depression. When couples learn in the therapy room that silence is not dangerous, that their words are not being tested, that their emotions are valid, they carry that learning into their daily lives. Arguments outside the room begin to shift. Instead of cross-examining each other, they learn to pause. Instead of demanding answers, they learn to ask fewer but better questions.

I sometimes use the metaphor of gardening to describe this. Curiosity is like water. Too little, and the soil stays dry. Too much, and the roots drown. The right amount allows growth. In the same way, the right question at the right time nourishes insight. But flooding clients with questions leaves them gasping for air. Our role is not to saturate, but to nurture.

When couples learn this principle themselves, it transforms their conversations. One partner says, "Why are you always so defensive?" — unhelpful. But if they slow down and instead ask, "What happens for you when I raise that issue?" the atmosphere shifts. The first question attacks. The second invites. The difference is not only relational — it's neurological. The attacking question triggers fight-or-flight. The invitational question engages reflection and calms the nervous system.

I often remind counsellors that less is best is not about doing less work. It's about doing more meaningful work. A well-placed question followed by silence can uncover layers of a person's history. A scatter of shallow questions might gather details but miss the heart. Clients don't need us to interrogate them into revelation. They need us to create space where their own insights can surface safely.

This takes trust in the process. It requires us to tolerate silence, to resist the urge to fill gaps, and to believe that insight can emerge slowly. For some of us, especially those new to counselling, this can feel excruciating. But silence is not a failure. It is a fertile pause. It is the nervous system recalibrating, the psyche gathering courage, the heart finding words it has never spoken before. If we can sit with that, we give our clients one of the greatest gifts possible: the experience of being safe enough to unfold.

By the time couples begin to practise observation, curiosity, validation, and restraint in the therapy room, something subtle but profound starts to change. The atmosphere softens. The sharp edges of blame give way to gentler tones. Partners who once looked at each other as adversaries start to glimpse themselves again as allies. This shift is not magic — it is neuroscience. Safety calms the nervous system. Recognition eases shame. Curiosity interrupts anxiety. These are not just communication techniques. They are interventions in mental health.

I think often of the way couples arrive at counselling exhausted. The endless fights, the quiet silences, the unspoken fears have worn them down. Depression often lingers in the background, whispering that nothing will ever change. Anxiety hovers in the room, each partner waiting for the next explosion or the next withdrawal. When they first walk in, their shoulders are tight, their voices quick, their eyes guarded. The nervous system is braced for threat.

What these couples need is not a barrage of clever tools but a space where their minds and bodies can finally breathe. Observation, curiosity, validation, and restraint combine to create that space. The counsellor notices the signals others have missed. Curiosity invites exploration rather than judgement. Validation soothes the raw edges of shame. Restraint ensures that silence is respected, not feared. Together, these elements build safety — and safety is the prerequisite for healing.

Take the example of Anna and Rob, who came into counselling on the verge of separation. Anna felt unheard and unvalued. Rob felt constantly criticised. Their sessions began with rapid back-and-forth accusations, each one louder and sharper than the last. My instinct at first was to ask questions, to slow them down, to intervene. But I remembered the principle of less is best. So instead of filling the space with questions, I began by observing.

"I notice both of you are speaking faster and louder as you describe this. What's happening inside as your voices rise?" Silence followed. Then Anna said quietly, "My chest is tight. I feel like he's not listening, so I push harder." Rob added, "When she pushes, I feel cornered. My head spins, and I want to shut down."

That exchange might sound simple, but it was monumental for them. It was the first time they had named what their bodies were doing in conflict. Anxiety and shutdown were no longer invisible enemies. They were spoken aloud, shared, and validated. From there, we could begin to work with them.

Validation became the bridge. "Anna, it makes sense that you'd push harder if you feel ignored. Many people do. And Rob, it makes sense that you'd feel overwhelmed and want to retreat if the intensity rises." Neither felt judged. Neither felt pathologised. Instead, they felt understood. Depression had been telling Anna she was unlovable.

Shame had been telling Rob he was weak. Validation pushed back against both lies.

From there, curiosity deepened the work. "Anna, what would feel more helpful than pushing when you feel unheard?" She paused, then said, "If he could just say, 'I hear you, give me a second to respond,' I wouldn't feel so desperate." I turned to Rob. "And what would feel more helpful than shutting down when you feel cornered?" He replied, "If she could lower her voice, I'd be able to stay in the room."

These weren't dramatic breakthroughs. They were small shifts in language and behaviour. But those small shifts had outsized effects on mental health. Anna's anxiety lessened when she was acknowledged. Rob's shame eased when he was validated. They both began to experiment with new ways of responding, and each success built hope. Hope, in turn, is one of the most protective factors in mental health.

What I've learned is that couples rarely need dozens of techniques. They need space to see each other differently, and they need guidance on how to respond in ways that soothe rather than inflame. Observation tells us where to look. Curiosity helps us ask the questions that matter. Validation reassures the nervous system that feelings make sense. Restraint keeps the process gentle. Each of these is simple, but together they are transformative.

For counsellors, the challenge is often internal. We live in a culture that values productivity and output. Silence feels like failure. Doing less feels like not doing enough. Yet in the therapy room, silence is fertile. Doing less allows more to emerge. Clients don't need us to rescue them with endless questions. They need us to stay with them long enough for the truth to surface. This requires patience and trust — trust in them, and trust in ourselves.

This is where Rogers' influence is so steadying. His emphasis on empathy, congruence, and unconditional positive regard reminds us that the conditions of the relationship are often more important than the content of the conversation. Empathy means listening beneath the words. Congruence means being honest about what we notice, even when it feels risky. Positive regard means holding clients in dignity, even when their behaviour looks messy. These principles are not outdated — they are anchors. They stop us from overcomplicating what can remain profoundly simple.

The mental health dimension of this is easy to underestimate. Couples who feel unsafe with each other live in chronic stress. Their nervous systems rarely rest. Sleep is disrupted. Energy is drained. Resentment grows. Over time, this chronic stress contributes to anxiety, depression, and even physical illness. By contrast, when couples feel safe, validated, and understood, their bodies relax. The parasympathetic nervous system engages. They sleep better. They cope better. Their capacity for joy returns. This is not only relationship counselling — it is health care.

It's worth noting, too, that observation and curiosity extend beyond words. I sometimes ask couples to notice what happens in their bodies during arguments. "Where do you feel it when you argue about money?" One might say, "In my stomach, it churns." The other might say, "In my shoulders, they tense up." Naming these bodily responses turns vague overwhelm into tangible information. It externalises what feels unbearable. Couples who learn to name their body's signals gain a tool for self-regulation, which directly supports mental health.

In the end, the essence of this chapter is not about filling the room with techniques, but about creating space where couples can be seen, heard, and validated. Observation, curiosity, validation, and restraint are not glamorous. They won't win awards for innovation. But they build safety, and safety builds healing.

I often leave sessions reflecting on how simple the shift can be. A counsellor notices. A partner pauses. A feeling is validated. A silence is honoured. These are the small hinges that swing big doors. And behind those doors is relief, regulation, and hope.

CHAPTER 3

THE ART OF ASKING QUESTIONS

Questions are the currency of counselling. They are the bridge we use to cross from surface stories into the deeper landscapes of meaning. But like currency, their value depends on how they are used. A coin can buy food, but it can also be thrown as a weapon. Questions, too, can nourish or wound.

Many couples who arrive at counselling are already raw from years of being questioned. "Why are you always like this?" "Why can't you just change?" "Why don't you care about me?" These are not neutral inquiries. They are indictments dressed up as curiosity. They leave behind a trail of shame and defensiveness. When a partner lives with anxiety or depression, these questions can land like blows. Anxiety hears them as confirmation that something is wrong. Depression hears them as proof of failure. Trauma hears them as echoes of old accusations.

When counsellors enter the picture, the danger is that we replicate the same dynamic without realising it. We pepper clients with questions, eager to demonstrate curiosity, but what they hear is interrogation. It is the difference between a doctor asking, "Can you tell me where it hurts?" and a customs officer barking, "Where are you coming from? What are you carrying?" The first invites honesty. The second demands compliance.

I recall working with a couple, David and Eliza, who had been together nearly twenty years. They were polite but distant, each sitting at opposite ends of the couch. I launched into my usual repertoire of open questions: "How did you meet? What first drew you to each other? What brings you here today?" They answered dutifully, but their bodies remained stiff, their eyes cast down. At the time, I told myself they were guarded. Later, reflecting, I realised I had made them feel like they were being interviewed, not invited into a conversation.

The distinction is subtle but crucial. An interview extracts information. A conversation shares meaning. Counselling is not about gathering data points. It is about creating space for clients to connect with themselves and with each other in ways they haven't before. My mistake with David and Eliza was to treat them like respondents in a survey rather than two human beings in pain.

This is where the mental health frame matters. People who live with depression are often carrying the unspoken story, "I am a failure." Every question that hints at performance — "Why haven't you tried this?" "What stops you from doing that?" — risks reinforcing that story. People who live with anxiety often carry the story, "Something terrible will happen if I get this wrong." Rapid-fire questions reinforce the sense of pressure and danger. Trauma survivors may carry the story, "I am not safe." A barrage of probing questions feels like intrusion, not care.

The art of asking questions begins with remembering that every nervous system in the room is listening. A question is not just words — it is an invitation or a threat, depending on tone, pace, and context. Even the simplest question can soothe or sting. "What do you need right now?" spoken gently with genuine care, is an opening. "Why do you always need so much?" spoken sharply, is a closing. Same subject, different impact.

I often explain to counsellors that a good question is less about clever phrasing and more about intention. If your question comes from a place of wanting to understand, it will usually land safely. If it comes from a place of wanting to control, prove, or fix, it will usually land poorly. Clients sense the difference instantly.

This doesn't mean we avoid difficult questions. Some of the most transformative moments in therapy come when a question stops a client in their tracks. But these questions only work if the groundwork of safety has already been laid. Without safety, the same question can retraumatise. With safety, it can open new possibilities. It is the difference between yanking open a locked door and gently knocking until someone chooses to let you in.

An example comes to mind with a couple I'll call Mark and Jess. Their relationship was strained after Jess discovered Mark had been secretly gambling. Jess was furious. Mark was defensive. The air in the room was thick with accusation. At one point, Jess turned to me and said, "Why does he keep lying? Why can't he just stop?" The temptation was to join her line of questioning and turn to Mark: "Why did you lie?" Instead, I paused and asked a different question: "What did gambling give you that nothing else did?"

The silence was heavy. Mark's shoulders dropped. He said quietly, "It made me feel calm. It shut my head up. When I stopped, the anxiety came back, and I couldn't cope." That was the first honest sentence he had spoken all session. Jess's face softened. She still hated what he had done, but for the first time, she understood what he was running from. My question had not absolved him, but it had shifted the frame from blame to cause. That shift is where mental health enters the story. Gambling wasn't the enemy. Anxiety was.

Good questions do this — they reframe. They move the focus from "What's wrong with you?" to "What's happened to you?" They help couples see that symptoms — secrecy, avoidance, anger — are often strategies for coping with stress, trauma, or fear. Once that link is made, compassion grows. Compassion doesn't erase accountability, but it makes accountability bearable.

The other trap with questions is assuming that more is better. Inexperienced counsellors often believe that if they just keep asking, eventually they will stumble on the magic question that unlocks everything. But couples are not safes to be cracked. They are people who need time to feel safe enough to reveal themselves. The art is not in asking ten questions but in asking one and then letting silence do its work.

Silence is terrifying for many counsellors. It feels like nothing is happening. But often, silence is where the most profound work is taking place. The nervous system is recalibrating. Memories are surfacing. Emotions are gathering courage to be spoken. If we rush to fill the silence with another question, we cut off that process. Sometimes the best question is the one we don't ask.

There is also the issue of ownership. Questions can sometimes hand responsibility back to the counsellor instead of leaving it with the client. If we ask too much, clients begin to look to us for answers, as though we are examiners holding the keys to their future. This dynamic undermines autonomy. Couples who already feel powerless — often a hallmark of depression and trauma — can become even more dependent. Our role is not to take ownership of their story but to help them reclaim it. Asking fewer, better questions honours their agency.

I often use the image of a lantern to describe this. A good question is like a lantern in the dark. It doesn't drag someone forward. It doesn't flood them with blinding light. It simply casts enough glow for them to see the next step. Clients don't need us to illuminate the entire path all at once. They need us to hold the lantern steady so they can walk it themselves.

The mental health benefits of this approach are real. People with anxiety learn that they don't need to have the perfect answer instantly. People with depression learn that their words have value even when they come slowly. Trauma survivors learn that their pace is respected, that they will not be pushed faster than they can go. These lessons restore dignity. They build resilience. They turn the counselling room into a place where nervous systems can rest instead of brace.

Asking questions, then, is not just a technique. It is a way of regulating the emotional climate. Done poorly, it escalates shame, fear, and defensiveness. Done well, it creates space for reflection, compassion, and change. The art is not in asking more, but in asking wisely, gently, and with full awareness of the stories and scars that sit behind every response.

If the first lesson in the art of asking questions is to do less, the second is to do it differently. Not all questions are created equal. Some slam the door shut. Others open it gently. The difference is not always in the wording, but in the intention, the pacing, and the way they land in the nervous system.

Interrogative questions are sharp, demanding, and often laced with frustration. They tend to begin with "why" and carry a tone of judgement. "Why did you do that?" "Why can't you ever listen?" "Why are you always so defensive?" These questions feel like cross-examinations, and most of us know what it's like to be on the receiving end of one. Your pulse quickens, your defences go up, and your mind scrambles to protect itself. Instead of reflection, you produce justification. Instead of honesty, you give whatever answer will keep you safe. Couples in conflict use these questions all the time, and the result is predictable: escalation, shame, withdrawal.

Invitational questions feel completely different. They lean in with gentleness, signalling openness rather than accusation. "Can you help me understand what was happening for you in that moment?" "What does it feel like when that happens?" "Would you be willing to share what this means to you?" These are not just softer versions of the same content. They reframe the entire dynamic. They say, "I'm curious about you" instead of "I'm against you." They slow down the body rather than speed it up. They create room for vulnerability.

I worked with a couple, Nadia and Paul, who illustrate this beautifully. Nadia often accused Paul of being cold and detached. He, in turn, accused her of being needy and relentless. When I asked Paul, "Why don't you show her more affection?" he bristled and crossed his arms. The session ground to a halt. Later, I tried again, but differently. "What happens for you inside when Nadia reaches for affection?" This time, his eyes welled up. He admitted, "I panic. I love her, but touch reminds me of when my father used to grab me in anger. I go numb before I can think." That moment cracked something open. The difference was not in Paul suddenly deciding to trust me. The difference was in the question. One accused. The other invited.

For Nadia, hearing his answer was a revelation. For years she had assumed his distance was rejection. Now she saw it as trauma. Her anxiety softened. She began to validate his fear rather than attack it. Paul, in turn, began to risk more touch, not because he was coerced, but because he felt understood. A single invitational question had shifted the entire frame, improving not only their relationship but also their mental health. Anxiety, shame, and loneliness had all eased within minutes.

The science backs this up. Research on trauma shows that accusatory "why" questions tend to trigger the amygdala, the brain's alarm system. When the alarm is blaring, the body goes into fight, flight, or freeze. Invitational questions, by contrast, activate the prefrontal cortex, the part of the brain associated with reflection and regulation. This is why the tone of our questions matters as much as the content. We are not just gathering information — we are shaping neurobiology in the room.

Refining our questioning style also means being mindful of sequence. Some questions are too big for the beginning. Clients need smaller, safer steps before they can face the hardest truths. Asking, "What does betrayal mean to you?" in the first session may be overwhelming. Asking, "What was the hardest part of that moment for you?" may be manageable. Over time, smaller questions build trust and prepare the ground for the bigger ones.

Restraint also plays a role here. Just because a question is good doesn't mean it's good right now. A couple's nervous system may be too activated for it to land safely. Part of the art is learning to hold a question for later. Sometimes I jot a phrase down on my notepad and return to it once the atmosphere has calmed. Timing can be the difference between breakthrough and shutdown.

Another refinement is the balance between closed and open questions. We are trained to favour open questions, and rightly so, but closed questions have their place. "Did you feel scared then?" can sometimes unlock honesty when "How did you feel?" is too broad. Clients who live with depression or trauma often struggle with expansive answers. A simple yes or no can be a relief. Once safety is established, open questions can follow. The key is flexibility, not dogma.

I remember a session with a young couple, Sarah and Mo. Mo struggled with depression, and Sarah often felt shut out. I asked Mo, "What do you need from Sarah when you're low?" He froze. The silence stretched painfully. Sensing his struggle, I shifted: "Do you need space, or do you need company?" His shoulders dropped with relief. "Company," he whispered. Sarah teared up. She had been giving him space, thinking that was what he wanted. The closed question had broken through where the open one had overwhelmed. From there, we could expand the conversation.

Questions can also become gifts when they are framed in the positive. Couples often talk in terms of what they don't want: "Don't nag me," "Stop ignoring me," "Quit yelling." Reframing the question towards the helpful makes a difference. "What helps you feel calmer when things get heated?" "What helps you feel closer after an argument?" These questions don't deny the pain, but they invite solutions. They shift the nervous system from defence to collaboration. For partners living with anxiety or depression, this feels radically different. Instead of being defined by their deficits, they are invited to explore their strengths.

Refining the art of questioning also means being transparent. Sometimes I tell clients why I'm asking something. "I'm asking this because I want to understand what's underneath the anger." That transparency builds trust. It reassures clients that I'm not prying for the sake of it. It models congruence, one of Rogers' core conditions, and demonstrates respect. Clients who live with trauma are especially sensitive to hidden agendas. Making the purpose clear protects them from suspicion and helps them settle.

The mental health benefits of this kind of questioning are immense. Anxiety decreases when questions feel invitational rather than accusatory. Depression lifts when clients are asked about what helps, not just about what hurts. Trauma symptoms ease when the pace, tone, and intention of questions signal safety. Couples who learn these styles of questioning themselves take them home. Instead of interrogating each other in the heat of conflict, they learn to ask gently, curiously, and transparently. Their arguments change not only in content but in physiology. Fewer alarms are triggered. More reflection is possible.

For me, the art of asking questions is really the art of building safety. Every time I ask something, I try to imagine how it will land in the body. Will it tighten the chest, or loosen it? Will it send the heart racing, or help it slow? Will it flood the mind with shame, or create space for compassion? These are not abstract considerations. They are the difference between therapy that retraumatises and therapy that heals.

This is why good counselling is less about having the perfect model and more about embodying presence. The best question is the one asked from a place of genuine care, paced with sensitivity, framed with transparency, and followed by enough silence for the answer to breathe. Anything less risks becoming another layer of pressure for clients who already carry too much. Anything more risks overwhelming them with expectations they cannot meet.

In the end, questions are not about us as counsellors. They are about the people in front of us, with their fragile nervous systems, their hidden histories, their desperate hopes. If we remember that, our questions become less like weapons and more like lanterns. They light the path without forcing the pace. They guide, they invite, and they heal.

The temptation to overuse questions is strongest when we, as counsellors, feel anxious ourselves. Silence stretches on, and something inside us panics: "I need to fill this. I need to do something." So we reach for another question, then another, until the session begins to sound less like a conversation and more like an interrogation. I've been guilty of this more than once, particularly in my early days. I thought curiosity meant keeping the dialogue alive at all costs. What I didn't realise was that my anxiety-driven questions were overwhelming my clients, pulling them further into defence instead of deeper into reflection.

This is one of the pitfalls of questioning: it can soothe the counsellor more than the client. We ask because it makes us feel active, useful, in control. But usefulness isn't measured by how many questions we ask. It's measured by whether those questions lead to safety, insight, and connection.

Another pitfall is assuming that questions are always neutral. They're not. Every question carries a tone, a pace, and an implied meaning. "Why did you do that?" may sound curious in our heads, but in the client's body it can land as judgement. For someone living with depression, that question reinforces the internal chorus of failure. For someone living with trauma, it echoes the interrogations of childhood. For someone living with anxiety, it confirms the fear that they're about to be caught out. The words might be the same, but the nervous system hears something else entirely.

This is why I have come to embrace the principle of "less is best." It is not a call to laziness but a call to precision. A single question, asked with care, can carry more weight than a dozen fired in succession. Less is best because it leaves room for silence, and silence is where nervous systems settle. Less is best because it allows clients to reach their own conclusions rather than being led down a path by the counsellor's agenda. Less is best because it prevents us from drowning people in curiosity when what they need is validation.

I worked with a couple, Fiona and Sam, who were caught in a painful loop. Fiona accused Sam of never opening up. Sam accused Fiona of interrogating him. In one session, she turned to him and said, "Why won't you tell me how you feel? Why are you always so shut down? Why can't you just talk to me like a normal person?" Each question was fuelled by desperation, but the effect was predictable. Sam's body stiffened, his eyes glazed, and his silence grew heavier.

We slowed it down together. I asked Fiona, "What happens inside you when Sam doesn't answer?" She said, "I panic. I think he doesn't care. I feel abandoned." I turned to Sam and asked, "What happens inside you when Fiona asks those questions?" He said, "I feel like I'm back at school being told off. My mind goes blank. I feel useless." Neither was wrong. Both were responding to the questions in ways shaped by their histories. The problem was not curiosity. The problem was the delivery. Fiona's interrogative questions were flooding Sam's nervous system with shame. His silence, in turn, was flooding her nervous system with fear.

This is what over-questioning does. It amplifies the very dynamics couples are desperate to escape. Instead of creating understanding, it deepens misunderstanding. Instead of reducing stress, it heightens it. Instead of building safety, it corrodes it. For couples already living with the weight of psychosocial stressors — financial strain, work burnout, parenting pressures — another round of interrogation is the last thing their nervous systems need.

When we, as counsellors, model "less is best," we show couples a different way. Instead of bombarding each other with "why" questions, they learn to choose one good question and let it breathe. Instead of filling silence with noise, they learn to trust the pause. Instead of interrogating, they learn to invite. This isn't just good communication — it's mental health hygiene. It regulates anxiety, interrupts shame and reduces the depressive spiral of "I can never get it right."

The danger of poor pacing in questioning cannot be overstated. If we ask a client to go too deep too quickly, we risk destabilising them. A question like, "What does betrayal mean to you?" might sound insightful, but for a traumatised client it can be overwhelming. They may not have the resources to answer safely. The result is dissociation, panic, or shutdown. Less is best reminds us to respect pacing. We can always return to the deeper questions once trust and safety are stronger.

There's another subtle pitfall: using questions to rescue. Sometimes a client shares something painful, and we feel an urge to soften it with a question that changes the subject. "You mentioned feeling lonely... what about your work, is that going better?" On the surface, it looks like curiosity. Underneath, it's avoidance. It communicates, "Your pain is too much for me to sit with." For clients already battling loneliness or shame, this lands as confirmation that even here, in counselling, they are too much.

The art is to stay with what is raw. Instead of escaping into another question, we might mirror what they said: "You feel lonely." Then we let the silence do its work. That silence, held with compassion, validates the client's reality in a way no clever question could. It says, "I can bear this with you." For mental health, that is transformative. Loneliness shrinks in the presence of another who stays.

I sometimes use the metaphor of painting to explain this to counsellors. Each question is a brushstroke. Too many brushstrokes too quickly turn the canvas into a blur. One careful stroke at the right time creates clarity. A session is not about covering every inch of the canvas in an hour. It is about choosing the strokes that matter most and trusting the image will emerge over time.

Couples benefit when they learn this, too. I often encourage them to notice how many questions they fire at each other during arguments. "Why don't you ever listen? Why do you always twist things? Why can't you just stop?" These barrages rarely lead to understanding. They lead to defensive counterattacks. When couples learn to replace ten questions with one — "What do you need from me right now?" — their arguments shift from attack to connection. This reduces stress, stabilises mood, and builds resilience. It may not sound dramatic, but the ripple effects on mental health are profound.

For me, the guiding principle is this: questions should never outpace safety. If safety is thin, questions must be gentle, few, and well-spaced. If safety is strong, deeper questions can be asked, but still with care. Our role is not to expose for the sake of exposure but to uncover in ways that strengthen, not shatter.

As I reflect on my own practice, I've learned that the moments that changed the most for couples were rarely the ones where I asked a clever question. They were the moments where I asked one question, waited, and then held the silence long enough for the real answer to arrive. That patience, that restraint, is where healing begins.

The more I practise, the more I realise that asking questions is not primarily a technical skill. It is an attitude. It is the outworking of empathy, congruence, and unconditional positive regard — Rogers' core conditions brought to life in the form of words. Without those conditions, even the most carefully phrased question can fall flat. With them, even the simplest question can be transformative.

Empathy reshapes questions. When we step into a client's world, we stop asking, "Why did you do that?" and begin asking, "What was it like for you in that moment?" The difference lies in the stance we take. Empathy turns interrogation into invitation. Couples who feel misunderstood are often braced for attack. Empathic questions lower their shields. They communicate, "I want to feel this with you, not judge you from the outside." For clients managing anxiety, depression, or trauma, that shift can be life changing. They no longer feel like case studies under a microscope. They feel like human beings being accompanied.

Congruence shapes questions too. Clients can sense when we are asking something because we think we're supposed to, rather than because we genuinely care. When our questions are incongruent — when our words don't match our presence — they fall flat. But when we ask something out of genuine curiosity, even if the phrasing is imperfect, clients hear the truth underneath. They trust us, not because we are flawless, but because we are real. I sometimes catch myself saying, "I don't know if this is the right way to put it, but I'm wondering..." That honesty lands better than any polished script. Couples can handle imperfection. What they crave is authenticity. For mental health, that authenticity is regulating. It reassures the nervous system: "This person is here, they are real, and they are not pretending."

Unconditional positive regard is perhaps the hardest to embody in questions, and also the most crucial. Couples often arrive in counselling when they are at their worst: shouting, sulking, blaming, shaming. If our questions are laced with our own judgement, they will feel it instantly. "Why do you treat her like that?" may be factually accurate, but it communicates disdain. "What happens inside you when you respond that way?" communicates respect for the person's humanity, even while naming their behaviour. This is not about excusing harm. It is about refusing to reduce people to their lowest moments. That refusal itself is profoundly healing. For clients who already believe they are broken or unworthy, positive regard embedded in questions is like oxygen.

I once worked with a couple, Carla and Ben, who had come to me after months of vicious arguments. Carla was exhausted, Ben was angry, and both were convinced the other was the problem. Early in our work, I found myself struggling with Ben's tone. He often dismissed Carla's feelings with a sharp laugh or an eye roll. My instinct was to challenge him bluntly. Instead, I paused and asked, "What does it cost you to stay in that defensive place?" It was a risky question, but it came from a place of regard. I wasn't asking to catch him out. I was asking because I sensed the cost must be heavy. To my surprise, he softened. He admitted, "I feel like I'm drowning, and if I admit I'm scared, she'll leave me. So, I laugh instead." In that moment, Ben revealed the fear behind his bravado. Carla, hearing it, burst into tears. The question hadn't fixed their marriage, but it had cracked open compassion. That's the power of unconditional regard made tangible in a question.

This is where the art of questioning intersects most clearly with mental health. Clients arrive weighed down by the symptoms of stress, trauma, anxiety, and depression. The questions they are used to hearing — from partners, from bosses, sometimes even from doctors — reinforce the message that they are defective. In counselling, our questions must do the opposite. They must communicate: "You make sense. Your pain makes sense. Let's explore it together." When that message is received, something shifts physiologically. Shoulders drop. Breathing steadies. The nervous system moves from threat to safety. Questions become not a demand for performance but an invitation to healing.

Sometimes the most healing question is not a question at all. It is a statement framed with curiosity. "You seem to be carrying a lot right now." "It looks like that memory still lingers for you." These are not interrogations. They are openings. They invite the client to step in or step back, without pressure. Couples often respond to these gentle observations more deeply than to any direct question. They feel seen rather than examined.

I recall a session with Helen and Marcus. They had spent forty minutes circling around the same argument about parenting styles. I could feel my own frustration rising. Every instinct told me to ask a pointed question to break the loop. Instead, I said softly, "You both look exhausted." The silence that followed was thick. Helen whispered, "We are." Marcus nodded, his eyes glassy. That simple statement, framed like a question but free of demand, allowed them to acknowledge something neither had been able to admit. From there, the conversation turned, not to parenting techniques, but to their shared fatigue and the impact it was having on their mental health.

When I speak to counsellors, I sometimes say, "The question isn't: What should I ask next? The question is: How do I need to be for my next question to land safely?" If I am hurried, my questions will rush. If I am anxious, my questions will probe. If I am genuinely present, my questions will emerge with warmth. This is why self-reflection is vital. Our internal state is the soil from which our questions grow. Couples feel it instantly.

The art of asking questions, then, is not about perfect technique. It is about cultivating presence, embodying the core conditions, and trusting the process. When empathy, congruence, and regard are alive in us, our questions will follow naturally. They may not be clever. They may not be polished. But they will be human. And human questions, asked at the right time, in the right spirit, have a way of piercing defences that no script could.

For couples living under the strain of psychosocial stress — job insecurity, caregiving burdens, unresolved trauma — this is more than communication technique. It is mental health intervention. When questions regulate rather than escalate, couples' bodies learn new ways of being together. Their fights soften. Their shame diminishes. Their sense of safety increases. The counselling room becomes a rehearsal space for healthier interactions outside it. That is how the art of asking questions contributes not just to relationship health, but to mental health more broadly.

And if, on some days, we fumble our way through with imperfect questions, that is all right. What matters is not that we get it right every time. What matters is that our curiosity is genuine, our pace is respectful, and our presence is steady. Couples will forgive a clumsy question if they sense our care. They will not forgive polished interrogation without regard. The art lies not in asking many questions, but in asking the kind that allow people to breathe, reflect, and discover themselves anew.

CHAPTER 4

VALIDATION, EMPATHY & THE POWER OF LANGUAGE

Couples arrive in the counselling room with words already worn thin. They have spoken, shouted, texted, whispered, and sulked. They have said "always" and "never" so often that the words have become weapons. In their exhaustion, they sometimes look at me as if to say, "You make sense of it. You translate." What they don't always realise is that the real work is not in creating more words, but in reshaping how words are used. The difference between a relationship that crumbles and one that recovers is often found not in a dramatic act of love or betrayal but in the small shifts of language that change the emotional climate.

Validation is where that shift begins. Validation does not mean agreement, nor does it mean surrendering your own perspective. It means acknowledging the reality of the other person's experience without trying to argue them out of it. "You're wrong" is the fastest way to trigger defensiveness. "I can see this matters to you" is the fastest way to calm a nervous system on fire. Clients who live with anxiety or depression often tell me the hardest part of conflict is not the disagreement itself but the sense of being dismissed. When their partner says, "You're overreacting," the anxiety spikes. When their partner says, "Stop being so negative," the depression deepens. These phrases invalidate not only the moment but the person's very way of experiencing the world. Invalidation is not neutral — it is corrosive. It worsens mental health because it tells someone, in essence, "What you feel isn't real."

I worked with a couple, Victor and Nancy, who illustrated this perfectly. Nancy struggled with low-level depression that he often masked with humour. Nancy had grown frustrated with what she saw as his lack of drive. "You never take things seriously," she would say. "It's like talking to a brick wall." Each comment landed like a stone on Victor's back. He withdrew further, leaving her angrier, which in turn pushed him deeper into silence. What broke the cycle was not a new strategy but a change in language. One evening in session, Nancy said, "It must feel heavy to carry that sadness all the time." Victor looked up, surprised. For the first time, he felt seen rather than criticised. The content of the conflict hadn't changed — he was still struggling with motivation — but the language had. That validation didn't fix his depression, but it shifted the relationship into a place where recovery could grow.

Empathy takes validation a step further. Validation says, "I see you." Empathy says, "I'm trying to feel this with you." It is the difference between standing on the bank watching someone struggle in the river and wading in to hold them as they fight the current. Couples who practise empathy begin to soften towards one another. When one partner can say, "I don't fully understand, but I can imagine how painful this is," the other partner's nervous system begins to calm. This is more than comfort. It is regulation. Anxiety quiets when it is met with empathy. Depression lifts slightly when it is met with compassion. Trauma begins to loosen its grip when it is met with steady presence. Empathy is medicine for the nervous system.

The challenge, of course, is that empathy requires slowing down. In arguments, couples rarely slow down long enough to ask, "What is this like for you?" They are too busy defending themselves or launching counter-attacks. When I coach couples to practise empathy, it can feel awkward at first. They roll their eyes. They say it sounds "scripted." But when they take the risk, the impact is immediate. The simple act of reflecting back a partner's words with warmth — "So when I stay late at work, you feel forgotten, like you don't matter" — can stop a fight in its tracks. The partner feels not only heard but cared for. That moment is often the first crack where light can get in.

The power of language becomes even clearer when we look at the difference between criticism and request. Criticism says, "You never help me." Request says, "It would help me if you took the bins out tonight." The first fuels shame and defensiveness. The second offers clarity and an opportunity for change. For couples already carrying stress or trauma, criticism often confirms their worst fears: "I'm failing, I'm hopeless, I'm a bad partner." Requests, by contrast, invite them into collaboration. They restore agency. They show that change is possible without dismantling identity.

In a session with Priya and Tom, who were constantly at war over household tasks. Priya would say, "You don't care about me. You never notice what I do." Tom would retreat, muttering, "I can't win with you." I introduced the shift from criticism to request. Priya tried: "It would help me if you loaded the dishwasher tonight." Tom blinked. "That, I can do," he said. It sounded almost too simple, but it was revolutionary. What changed was not the chore but the frame. The request removed the sting of accusation and gave Tom a clear path to show care. Over time, this small shift in language reduced the atmosphere of constant blame and began to rebuild trust. The effect on both their mental states was striking. Priya's resentment eased. Tom's sense of failure lifted.

This is why I talk about language as a tool for mental health. Words are not just communication devices. They are nervous system regulators. They can inflame or soothe, constrict or expand. A raised voice and sharp tone can send an anxious partner into fight-or-flight. A calm statement of validation can lower the stress and steady breathing. Couples often underestimate this. They think words are "just words." But when you see how bodies respond in session — the dropped shoulders, the slower breathing, the softened gaze — you realise language is physiology in action.

As counsellors, we model this. The way we frame our own language in session teaches couples how to speak differently to each other. If a partner says, "He's useless," I might gently reframe: "It sounds like you're saying you feel unsupported." That subtle shift shows them that their experience can be expressed without shaming the other. Over time, couples begin to internalise these reframes. They start to catch themselves mid-sentence, moving from "You never" to "It would help me if." That is language doing its quiet work of repair.

But language can also betray us when we are careless. Even counsellors sometimes slip into phrases that wound. I remember early in my practice saying to a client, "Why don't you just try to…" Her face fell. She later told me she felt judged, as though I believed she wasn't trying hard enough. I hadn't intended to shame her, but my words carried that weight. Since then, I've learned to check myself. If my language risks sounding dismissive or prescriptive, I stop. Instead of "Why don't you try," I now say, "Would you be open to exploring…" The meaning is similar, but the tone is worlds apart.

This carefulness with language is not about being artificially polite. It is about creating conditions where the most fragile parts of a person can come forward. When a client tells me about their depression, I do not say, "You should think more positively." That would shut them down. I say, "It sounds like life feels very heavy right now." That validation doesn't solve the depression, but it tells them they are not alone with it. That, in itself, is a form of treatment.

What makes this work so profound is that couples take it home. They begin to notice the difference between helpful and unhelpful phrases. They replace, "You're overreacting" with, "I can see this is hard for you." They trade, "You never care" for, "I'd feel cared for if…" These may look like tiny edits, but they are seismic shifts in the emotional climate. Over time, the accumulation of small validations, small empathic reflections, and small requests reshape the relationship. That reshaping, in turn, improves each partner's mental health. Anxiety decreases when the nervous system is met with steady empathy. Depression eases when validation replaces dismissal. Trauma heals when language signals safety instead of danger.

In many ways, language is the bloodstream of a relationship. If the language is toxic — filled with criticism, contempt, or invalidation — the whole body of the relationship grows sick. If the language is nurturing — filled with validation, empathy, and constructive requests — the relationship becomes healthier, stronger, more resilient. Couples who learn this find that arguments still happen, but they no longer devastate. They become manageable, survivable, even connective. That is the power of language at work.

When I first invite couples to practise validation and empathy in session, the reaction is often a groan. They look at me with suspicion, as if I've just asked them to rehearse lines in a bad play. Some even laugh nervously. "You want me to repeat that back to him?" "That sounds fake." "She'll think I'm mocking her." The resistance is predictable, and in some ways, it's reassuring. It tells me I'm asking them to try something outside their normal pattern. Patterns are comfortable, even when they're destructive. Stepping into empathy feels unnatural precisely because invalidation has become second nature.

This is where I remind couples that new skills always feel clumsy at first. Think about learning to drive. At the beginning, every action feels mechanical. You grip the wheel too tightly, check the mirrors obsessively, stall the engine. Over time, it becomes second nature. The same is true of empathy and validation. At first, the words sound wooden, forced. But with repetition, they begin to soften, and eventually they become habits that reshape the relationship.

The awkwardness is also a reflection of vulnerability. Saying, "I can see this hurts you," requires lowering the shield. For some clients, particularly those carrying trauma or shame, that openness feels dangerous. To acknowledge another's pain is to risk being pulled into it. To acknowledge one's own role in causing it is to risk confronting guilt. So instead they reach for sarcasm, laughter, or silence. The work of counselling is not to scold them for resisting but to normalise the discomfort and invite them to practise anyway.

I remember a couple, Matthew and Elise, who struggled with validation. Elise often accused Matthew of dismissing her feelings. Matthew would defend himself: "I don't dismiss you, I just don't agree with you." In one session, after a heated exchange, I asked Matthew to try validation instead. "Can you tell Elise you see how important this is to her?" He rolled his eyes. "Fine. I see it's important." Elise bristled. "That's not real." She was right — it wasn't. But rather than abandon the exercise, we paused and unpacked it. Matthew admitted that saying those words made him feel like he was giving up his position, like he was surrendering. For him, validation equalled defeat. Once he realised validation was not agreement but acknowledgement, he relaxed. The next attempt was softer: "I don't fully understand why this matters so much, but I can see that it really does matter to you." Elise's face softened. She felt heard, even though he hadn't changed his stance. The language hadn't just changed the conversation — it had changed their physiology.

This is the key point for counsellors: validation is not about solving the problem. It is about regulating the nervous system. Couples cannot problem-solve when they are flooded with anger or fear. Validation lowers the temperature enough for constructive conversation to happen. From a mental health perspective, this is huge. Anxiety is soothed when it feels seen. Depression lifts when despair is acknowledged. Trauma loses its intensity when pain is named rather than denied. Validation isn't just a communication skill; it's medicine for shame. Shame tells people, "You're broken. You don't matter. You'll never get it right." When shame runs the show, every disagreement becomes proof of failure. Validation interrupts that script. It says, "You make sense. Your feelings matter. You are still worthy, even in conflict." That single shift can turn a couple from adversaries into allies.

Empathy works the same way. I often ask couples to swap perspectives in session. One speaks, the other mirrors back what they heard, not just in content but in feeling. "So you felt scared when I raised my voice." "You felt alone when I stayed at work late." At first, it sounds stilted. Sometimes they laugh in embarrassment. But then, something shifts. When a partner hears their own feelings reflected back with care, the nervous system relaxes. It is as though the body whispers, "Finally. Someone gets it." That recognition is powerful enough to soften even the deepest anger.

Not every couple embraces this quickly. Some resist with sarcasm. I recall one husband who, when asked to reflect back his wife's words, said flatly, "So you feel sad. Great. Noted." His wife burst into tears. I gently intervened, asking him to slow down and try again, this time imagining how he would want someone to speak to him if he were hurting. He sighed, then said, "I didn't realise how lonely you felt. That must be awful." The difference was immediate. His wife looked up at him stunned. "That's the first time you've ever said that." In that moment, years of distance narrowed. The words themselves were simple. The empathy in his tone was what made them transformative.

This is why I tell couples that validation and empathy are not about finding the perfect phrase. They are about intention. The nervous system is less interested in eloquence than in authenticity. You don't need to be poetic. You need to be present. Even clumsy words, if spoken with genuine care, regulate better than polished phrases spoken with indifference.

The resistance to practising empathy also reveals how couples often confuse empathy with agreement. They worry that if they validate the other's experience, they are conceding the argument. This is a false dichotomy. You can empathise without agreeing. You can say, "I understand you felt hurt" without saying, "I agree I was wrong." Couples who learn this distinction find that their fights become less about scoring points and more about building bridges. The relief is palpable. For clients managing mental health challenges, this relief is more than emotional. It is physiological. Fewer fights mean fewer spikes of cortisol, fewer nights of sleepless rumination, fewer spirals of despair.

Practising validation also requires learning the difference between empathy and pity. Pity looks down; empathy stands alongside. When a partner says, "Poor you," it reinforces helplessness. When a partner says, "That must be painful for you," it honours strength as well as struggle. This distinction matters deeply for clients with depression. Pity feeds the sense of inadequacy. Empathy affirms resilience. The words may be similar, but the posture is worlds apart.

For counsellors, coaching this practice requires patience. Couples often need to experiment, fail, and try again. The first attempts may sound hollow. The second may backfire. But with persistence, something shifts. I often liken it to learning a new language. At first, you stumble over the grammar. Then, slowly, you begin to think in the new tongue. Eventually, it becomes natural. The language of empathy is no different.

And the impact extends beyond the counselling room. Couples who practise validation at home begin to notice changes in daily interactions. A wife says, "You're always on your phone." Instead of snapping back, the husband says, "I can see that makes you feel ignored." The tension diffuses. A husband says, "You don't want to visit my family." Instead of defending, the wife says, "I understand this feels important to you." The argument never escalates. The nervous systems regulate before they spiral. Over weeks and months, these small moments accumulate, reshaping the emotional climate of the relationship. That reshaping has direct effects on mental health. Anxiety reduces because the threat level drops. Depression lightens because despair is not left in isolation. Trauma heals because safety is reinforced in small, steady doses.

I explain to couples that validation and empathy are like tending a garden. The soil of a relationship may be depleted from years of conflict. Each act of validation is like adding compost. Each moment of empathy is like watering the roots. At first, nothing seems to change. The ground still looks barren. But over time, the soil becomes fertile again, and new growth emerges. That growth is not dramatic, but it is sustainable. For couples dealing with psychosocial stressors, this steady growth is often the difference between survival and collapse.

The hardest part for many couples is breaking the habit of invalidation. "You're overreacting." "That's ridiculous." "Here we go again." These phrases roll off the tongue without thought. Part of our role as counsellors is to help them notice these defaults and replace them with alternatives. I sometimes ask couples to keep a journal of unhelpful phrases they catch themselves saying. Then we brainstorm together to find validating alternatives. It sounds simple, but the act of noticing is half the battle. Once awareness grows, change follows.

For counsellors, the same principle applies. We, too, can slip into invalidating language without meaning to. "Why don't you just try..." "You need to stop..." These phrases may be intended as encouragement but land as criticism. The discipline of practising validation in our own language — with clients and with ourselves — strengthens our presence. It reminds us that the goal is not to fix but to accompany.

In the end, practising validation and empathy is less about technique and more about courage. It takes courage to lower defences, to risk being misunderstood, to sit with another's pain without rushing to solutions. But when couples take that risk, they discover a new way of relating that not only heals the relationship but also supports their mental health. They move from adversaries to allies, from invalidation to compassion, from despair to hope. And it all begins with words spoken differently — words that heal instead of harm.

Language is not just about the words themselves; it's about the tone, the timing, and the emotional weight that carries them. I've sat in sessions where a partner says the right words but delivers them with a flat voice or a sharp edge, and the effect is lost. "I'm sorry you feel that way" can sound like compassion in one tone and contempt in another. Couples sometimes underestimate just how much their nervous systems respond to these subtleties. For a partner already carrying anxiety or trauma, tone matters as much as content. Their body hears sarcasm as threat. Their mind reads indifference as abandonment. A flat or cutting delivery can undo the very validation we are trying to build.

This is why, when we work with couples, we cannot focus only on language as a cognitive exercise. It is embodied. The nervous system is always in the background, scanning for cues of safety or danger. A warm tone, eye contact, and an open posture can make the difference between a sentence landing as attack or as empathy. If a partner says,

"I can see this is hard for you," but does so while rolling their eyes, the message is not empathy — it is dismissal. The words are there, but the meaning is stripped away. For clients who already live with shame, this lands as confirmation: "Even when they try, I'm not worth taking seriously."

Humour is another subtle but powerful part of language. It can build bridges or burn them. Couples often use humour as a coping mechanism. A gentle joke can diffuse tension, remind partners of their bond, and bring a sense of relief. I've seen couples on the brink of tears who suddenly laugh at the absurdity of their dishwasher wars, and in that laughter, something softens. The nervous system shifts from fight to play. For mental health, that moment of playfulness is a protective factor — a reminder that even in struggle, joy is possible.

But humour can also wound. Sarcasm masquerades as wit but often functions as a blade. "Nice of you to finally show up on time," may get a laugh in a sitcom, but in a counselling room it's fuel on the fire. Sarcasm invalidates by cloaking criticism in a joke, leaving the other partner feeling both attacked and dismissed. For someone managing depression, sarcasm reinforces the sense of inadequacy. For someone living with trauma, it reinforces vigilance: every smile hides a jab. Part of our task is to help couples distinguish between humour that heals and humour that harms.

Metaphor is another layer of language that carries weight in counselling. I often use metaphors in my own work because they allow couples to step outside the rawness of their conflict and see it in a new light. I've described reactivity as a tennis match, stress as a fog, or conflict as a smoke alarm. Metaphors like these create distance. They externalise the problem so couples can unite against it rather than against each other. For mental health, this is invaluable. Anxiety lessens when problems feel nameable. Trauma softens when chaos is translated into imagery. Depression lifts slightly when despair is framed as fog — not permanent, just obscuring.

But metaphors can also misfire if they don't resonate. I once used a sailing metaphor with a couple who had never sailed. My words fell flat, and they stared at me blankly. It reminded me that language must always be tailored to the people in front of us. For some, a metaphor of sport makes sense; for others, art or nature connects better. The danger of misapplied metaphor is that it alienates rather than connects. The work is not about showing off clever imagery but about finding language that truly speaks to a couple's shared experience.

The subtlety of language is also evident in the difference between absolutes and specifics. Absolutes — "you always," "you never" — are poison to mental health in relationships. They trigger defensiveness and despair. For clients living with depression, "you never" confirms the belief that nothing they do is enough. For those with anxiety, "you always" amplifies the fear that they are perpetually failing. Shifting language to specifics changes the impact. "Last night, when you stayed at work late, I felt lonely" is worlds apart from "You never put me first." The first is grounded in reality and opens a door to empathy. The second locks the door with accusation.

I worked with a couple, Hannah and Luke, who illustrated this beautifully. Hannah often said to Luke, "You never listen." Luke would fold his arms and shut down, hearing it as proof of his inadequacy. One day, I coached Hannah to be specific. Instead of "You never listen," she said, "When I told you about my day yesterday and you kept looking at your phone, I felt invisible." Luke's shoulders dropped. He looked at her and said quietly, "I didn't realise how much that moment mattered." That small shift from absolute to specific turned a spiral of shame into a moment of connection. The content hadn't changed — the phone was still an issue — but the language had shifted the meaning.

Tone, humour, metaphor, and specificity may sound like minor details, but for couples living under the weight of psychosocial stressors, these details matter profoundly. Stress and trauma heighten sensitivity. The nervous system is already on alert, scanning for cues of safety or danger. A sarcastic joke lands harder. An absolute cuts deeper. A dismissive tone confirms fears. Conversely, a gentle tone, a shared laugh, a well-placed metaphor, or a specific phrase of validation can create safety. And safety is the soil in which mental health recovery grows.

As counsellors, we can model these subtleties. When a partner uses sarcasm, we can gently translate: "I hear the joke, but I also hear the pain underneath. Can you put that into words without the humour?" When absolutes arise, we can reframe: "Instead of 'always,' can you tell me about a recent moment that felt like that?" When tone undercuts content, we can reflect: "You said the words, but your voice sounded sharp. What was happening for you then?" These interventions are not about policing language but about teaching couples to notice its impact. Awareness is the first step toward change.

And here is where the mental health frame becomes vital. Language is not merely communication; it is co-regulation. Every phrase either calms or inflames, soothes or shames. When couples learn to attune to the power of tone, humour, metaphor, and specificity, they are not just improving communication — they are supporting each other's mental health. Anxiety finds safety in gentle tone. Depression finds dignity in validation. Trauma finds relief in humour that heals rather than harms. These are not small shifts. They are lifelines.

For counsellors, the lesson is clear: the art of language is not about technique alone. It is about presence, timing, and sensitivity. We may ask ourselves, "How will this phrase land in their body?" not just, "Does this phrase make sense?" When we bring that awareness to our own language and model it for couples, we create a ripple effect that extends beyond the session. Couples take it home. They begin to notice their own tones, their own metaphors, their own defaults to absolutes. Slowly, they replace harshness with gentleness, sarcasm with sincerity, absolutes with specifics. The mental health benefits accumulate like compound interest, steady and enduring.

In the end, the subtleties of language matter because people matter. Words are not neutral tools. They are carriers of meaning, memory, and emotion. They can confirm shame or interrupt it, deepen fear or soothe it, entrench despair or spark hope. Couples who learn this begin to see language not as ammunition but as medicine. And when that shift happens, the counselling room becomes not only a place of conversation but a place of healing.

By the time couples reach a place where validation and empathy begin to feel possible, the work is less about techniques and more about posture — not posture of the body, though that matters too, but posture of presence. The way we hold ourselves in the room, the way we respond to what is said, and the way we frame even the smallest responses can either cultivate trust or erode it.

I often think of Rogers here, not in the abstract but in the most practical sense. Empathy, congruence, and unconditional positive regard are not lofty ideals reserved for textbooks. They are visible in the very words we choose. They're present in whether we say, "Why did you do that?" or "What was it like for you then?" They're present in whether we sigh impatiently when a client circles back to the same story or whether we lean in and ask, "What feels unfinished about this for you?" Language is the delivery system for the core conditions. Without them, our words are just noise. With them, even the simplest phrase can change a life.

I once sat with a couple, Mark and Angela, who were on the edge of collapse. They had tried every communication tool, every self-help strategy, and nothing seemed to stick. In one session, Angela wept openly, saying she felt like she was failing as a wife and mother. Mark, defensive, muttered, "She's too sensitive." My instinct was to challenge him, but instead I turned my attention to Angela and said quietly, "You seem to be doing the best you can, even while feeling so overwhelmed." She broke down further, not from despair but from relief. She said later that no one had ever said those words to her before. For her, that simple phrase carried empathy, congruence, and positive regard. It validated her pain without pathologising it. It affirmed her effort without minimising her struggle. In that moment, she felt less alone.

For Mark, hearing those words had an effect too. He softened, realising that what he had dismissed as oversensitivity was actually the cry of someone stretched thin. His defensiveness lowered, and he asked her, for the first time in months, "What would help you right now?" That shift wasn't about a clever intervention. It was about language infused with presence. It demonstrated that sometimes the best way to model empathy is to speak the words aloud in the room so couples can see how it feels.

When couples learn this posture of language, they begin to practise it at home. They stop waiting for the counsellor to supply validation and start supplying it themselves. One partner says, "You're doing the best you can," and the other sighs with relief. These moments are not grand reconciliations. They are small, steady acts of repair. Over time, they accumulate. They become the new soundtrack of the relationship. And because shame is such a destructive force in mental health, these acts of validation become antidotes. They interrupt the internal script of "I'm failing, I'm broken" with the external affirmation of "You make sense."

It is worth noting that empathy expressed through language is not always verbal. Silence itself, if held with warmth, can be profoundly validating. Sometimes, when a partner finishes speaking, the other rushes in with, "I know exactly how you feel." This can be well-intentioned, but it often misses the mark. Silence, paired with attentive presence, communicates empathy in ways words cannot. The nervous system relaxes in the quiet, sensing no interruption, no correction, no hijacking of the story. For clients with trauma, silence can feel safer than any question. For those with depression, silence says, "I'm still here," when words might otherwise feel overwhelming.

The challenge for counsellors is to model that kind of silence. It requires resisting the urge to fill every gap with interpretation or technique. It means trusting that empathy does not always require language, though when language is used, it must be chosen carefully. This balance — between words and silence — is one of the most delicate arts of counselling. It is also one of the most protective for mental health. Clients learn that they are not pressured to produce, perform, or defend. They learn that they can simply be.

As sessions progress, language also becomes the arena where congruence is tested. Clients know when we're hiding behind jargon or cloaking our uncertainty in polished technique. They know when we're out of our minds — caught up in our own anxiety about "getting it right" rather than being present. When our language is congruent — when it matches our actual feelings and stance — it builds trust. Saying, "I don't have an immediate answer, but I'm with you in this," often lands better than a dozen theoretical formulations. For clients managing anxiety or shame, that congruence is profoundly regulating. It communicates, "You don't have to perform, and neither do I."

Unconditional positive regard shows up in our language when we refuse to let behaviour define worth. A partner may shout, sulk, or shut down. We can name the behaviour without stripping the person of dignity. "I hear that you shouted because you felt unheard" keeps worth intact while acknowledging impact. Compare this with, "You're being childish." One builds safety. The other deepens shame. For couples who already come in weighed down by the message that they are not good enough, our language must be the place where they hear a counter-narrative. It is not about excusing harm, but about insisting on humanity. That insistence is medicine.

The more I work with couples, the more I believe that the smallest linguistic shifts make the biggest difference. "You never" becomes "Last night, I felt." "Why are you like this?" becomes "What was it like for you?" "Stop overreacting" becomes "I can see this feels big for you." These are not tricks. They are acts of empathy in real time. They are ways of shaping the environment so that nervous systems can rest, so that shame can loosen its grip, so that love can find space to breathe again.

For counsellors, the invitation is clear. We don't need to have all the answers. We don't need to deliver speeches filled with insight. What we need is to let our language embody the conditions that heal: empathy that regulates, congruence that reassures, positive regard that restores dignity. If we can do that, we give couples something more valuable than any technique. We give them a living demonstration of what safe, caring language feels like. And once they've felt it, they can carry it with them into their own lives, replicating it with each other long after the counselling room is behind them.

When I think about the role of language in relationships, I often picture it as the atmosphere we breathe. Harsh words, sarcastic tones, invalidating phrases — these are like pollution in the air. They choke, they sicken, they exhaust. Gentle words, validating tones, empathic reflections — these are like clean oxygen. They nourish, they energise, they heal. Couples do not always notice the atmosphere they are breathing until it becomes toxic. Our task is to help them notice, and then to show them that they can change it. They can clear the air. They can choose words that make the space between them breathable again.

And when they do, something remarkable happens. Anxiety finds rest in calm tones. Depression eases under validating words. Trauma begins to heal when shame is met with unconditional regard. Language, so often taken for granted, becomes the very medium of recovery. This is not abstract theory. It is the lived experience of countless couples who discover that when they change the way they speak, they change the way they live. And for counsellors, there are few things more satisfying than witnessing that transformation take root, one careful word at a time.

CHAPTER 5

THE FOUR STAGES OF COMPETENCY: YES, EVERYONE STARTS OUT A LITTLE MUDDLED

When couples arrive in counselling, they are often caught in the first stage of competency: unconscious incompetence. Put simply, they don't yet know what they don't know. They sit across from each other, convinced that the problem is obvious — "He doesn't listen," or "She nags," or "We've grown apart." They're aware of the tension, the arguments, the distance, but they haven't yet understood the deeper causes. They believe that if only the other would change, the relationship would improve.

This is unconscious incompetence in relationships: not realising that the very patterns they are stuck in are part of the problem. It's not stupidity, and it's not wilful ignorance. It's human. Most of us start relationships with hope, attraction, and the vague sense that love will be enough. We aren't taught about attachment styles in school. No one hands us a guidebook on how trauma, stress, or unspoken expectations will weave themselves into daily life. Couples stumble into conflict thinking it's about the dishwasher, or the bills, or the sex, unaware that these are only the visible symptoms of something deeper.

The difficulty of this stage is that couples don't know they lack certain skills. They assume their way of seeing the world is universal. A partner raised in a home where emotions were suppressed may genuinely believe that silence is the respectful way to handle conflict. A partner raised in a loud, expressive household may believe the opposite — that raising your voice shows passion and commitment. Neither recognises that their approach is shaped by history. Each assumes the other is being difficult on purpose. The incompetence isn't malicious; it's unconscious.

From a mental health perspective, this stage can be profoundly destabilising. Anxiety spikes when couples misinterpret each other's behaviour as rejection. Depression deepens when partners feel perpetually misunderstood or unseen. Trauma is reactivated when old wounds are triggered but not recognised for what they are. Couples in unconscious incompetence are often locked in a reactive cycle, each partner responding to the surface symptoms without naming the underlying cause. The more they react, the more evidence they collect that the other is the problem. It's exhausting, confusing, and lonely.

I once worked with a couple — let's call them George and Karen — who embodied this stage perfectly. George would shut down during arguments, going quiet and withdrawn. Karen, desperate to reconnect, would chase after him, demanding answers. The more she pursued, the further he retreated. When they first came in, Karen said flatly, "He doesn't care about us. He just runs away." George countered, "She never stops. She just goes on and on." Both were convinced the other's behaviour was the problem. Neither realised they were caught in a pattern where both reactions made perfect sense once you knew their histories. George's silence was his nervous system's freeze response, a survival tactic from growing up in a home where conflict often became explosive. Karen's pursuit was her fear of abandonment, shaped by a childhood where being ignored meant being forgotten. They didn't yet know what they didn't know — that their cycle wasn't personal failure but nervous system survival.

This is why unconscious incompetence in relationships is so painful. Couples are genuinely baffled by why things keep going wrong. They try to apply surface solutions — rotating chores, setting rules, negotiating compromises — but the arguments persist. Without awareness, they are like drivers on a foggy road, convinced they're steering carefully but unaware they're heading straight for a ditch. They don't yet realise that the fog is not the partner, but the stress, the trauma, the old wounds clouding their vision.

For counsellors, the task in this stage is gentle education. Not lecturing, not overwhelming, but offering enough insight for couples to begin recognising the patterns they're in. This is where metaphors help. When I tell couples, "The dishwasher isn't about the dishwasher; it's the tip of the iceberg," they often pause, blink, and suddenly see the argument differently. When I say, "You're not fighting each other; you're both fighting stress, it just wears a different disguise for each of you," their faces soften. Awareness dawns. They begin to realise that what looked like incompetence in love was really unconsciousness of how their mental health histories shaped their reactions.

It's also important to frame this stage with compassion. Couples in unconscious incompetence often arrive carrying shame. They say, "We shouldn't need counselling. We should be able to sort this ourselves." Shame convinces them they're broken, that everyone else is managing relationships just fine. But shame thrives in silence, and part of our work is to normalise the muddle. To say, "Everyone starts here. You're not failing. You're just learning to see what's really going on."

In many ways, this stage is hopeful. Once couples become aware that there is more beneath the surface, they've already taken the first step toward growth. It's like the moment a learner driver realises there are blind spots. It's unnerving at first, but it's the awareness that keeps them safer in the long run. The couple begins to glimpse that their conflicts aren't proof of incompatibility, but signals of skills they haven't yet learned. That realisation alone can reduce anxiety, soften shame, and make room for curiosity.

This first stage reminds us that love isn't enough on its own. Relationships, like any skill, require learning. Unconscious incompetence is simply the beginning of that learning journey. And with guidance, compassion, and a focus on mental health, couples can move from not knowing what they don't know to seeing their patterns clearly. That clarity is the foundation on which change is built.

If unconscious incompetence is the fog of not knowing what you don't know, then conscious incompetence is when the fog lifts just enough for you to see the potholes — and the sight can be overwhelming. For couples, this stage often arrives with a jolt. They begin to realise that their arguments aren't just about chores or money or sex. They see the patterns, sometimes for the first time, and it can feel crushing.

This is the stage where partners say things like, "I know I'm being defensive, but I can't stop." Or, "I can see I'm shutting down, but I don't know how to do it differently." There is an emerging awareness that their behaviours are part of the cycle, not just the other person's fault. But that awareness doesn't come with an instruction manual. It's the difference between spotting the problem and knowing how to solve it. And in that gap, frustration often grows.

From a mental health perspective, this stage is where shame tends to roar the loudest. Shame tells couples, "You can see how you're failing, and you still can't fix it. You're broken. You're hopeless." Partners often leave sessions shaking their heads, saying, "We get it, but nothing changes." That despair can mimic depression, draining energy and hope. For those with trauma histories, conscious incompetence can reactivate old wounds: "I knew I'd never get it right. I always mess up." Awareness without skills can feel like standing in quicksand — the harder you struggle, the deeper you sink.

I remember working with a couple — let's call them Rachel and Adam — who embodied this stage perfectly. Rachel had a sharp tongue when she felt dismissed. Adam shut down when he felt criticised. In our early sessions, both blamed the other. But after a few weeks, something shifted. Rachel sighed one day and said, "I know I go for the jugular. I hear the words coming out, and I hate myself for saying them. But in the moment, I just can't stop." Adam nodded and admitted, "I know I withdraw. I see how it hurts her. But it's like my body freezes, and I can't move."

This was conscious incompetence: the painful awareness that they were part of the problem, coupled with the helplessness of not yet having another way to be. It was progress — far more progress than they realised — but it didn't feel like it. For them, it felt like failure.

As counsellors, one of our most important roles in this stage is to reframe it. Awareness is not failure. Awareness is movement. Couples often expect that once they see their patterns, change should be immediate. But human nervous systems don't work like that. Years of survival strategies don't vanish overnight. Conscious incompetence is like the learner driver who now knows about blind spots but still forgets to check them. The knowledge is there, but the habit hasn't formed. Mistakes aren't proof of hopelessness; they're proof of learning.

This is also where external stressors amplify the struggle. A couple might leave the session with new awareness but then walk straight into a week of work pressure, sick children, financial strain, or unresolved trauma. Their capacity is depleted, so they revert to old patterns. Awareness plus exhaustion equals relapse. From a mental health angle, this is entirely predictable. Couples aren't failing; they're flooded. When the nervous system is overwhelmed, even the best intentions collapse. Naming this reality can relieve some of the shame. It shifts the narrative from "We're useless" to "We're human, and stress is stretching us."

One of the metaphors I often use here is Newton's cradle — the row of silver balls that click back and forth. At this stage, the couple feels like the noisy ball in the middle. Every time they swing forward with good intentions, another ball swings back with old patterns. It feels noisy, repetitive, and endless. But the clicking isn't failure. It's motion. Conscious incompetence is noisy because the system is in transition. Change is happening, even if it's not yet visible.

What's vital in this stage is the counsellor's reassurance and pacing. Couples may arrive desperate for quick fixes. They want scripts, rules, guarantees. The danger is that we hand them tools as though they're magic bullets, which can actually deepen the shame when the tools don't work immediately. Instead, we normalise the struggle. We say, "This is the awkward stage. You're not supposed to get it right yet." That validation is medicine for shame. It reframes the mistakes as evidence of growth, not incompetence.

Take another example: a couple I'll call Leo and Hannah. Hannah had been reading about attachment theory and came into session declaring, "I know I'm anxious, and he's avoidant. I keep clinging, and he keeps running. I see it now, and I hate it." Leo sat quietly and said, "I know I run, but when she clings, I panic. I want to change, but I don't know how." Both of them had stepped into conscious incompetence. They could see the dance, name the roles, and even connect them to their histories. But they couldn't yet change the steps. They left that session looking defeated.

Here's the reframe I offered them: "The fact that you can both see the dance is huge. Most couples never get this far. You're not failing; you're learning the choreography. Right now, you'll trip, you'll step on each other's toes, you'll lose rhythm. That's normal. The point is you're not dancing blind anymore." Their shoulders dropped. The shame eased just enough for them to keep trying.

Mental health symptoms in this stage often mirror the relational stuckness. Anxiety spikes before conversations because partners anticipate falling into old traps. Depression whispers that the effort isn't worth it, that nothing will change. Trauma responses flare as partners relive helplessness from childhood. This is why it's essential to slow the process down. The goal isn't immediate perfection. The goal is tolerance — tolerance of mistakes, tolerance of discomfort, tolerance of not yet.

I sometimes suggest couples create a shared language for this stage. Instead of hurling accusations, they can name the process: "I think we're in our clumsy stage right now." This externalises the struggle. It's not "You're failing" or "I'm hopeless." It's "We're learning." That shift alone can reduce shame and increase resilience.

For counsellors, this is also a stage where our own patience is tested. It's easy to become frustrated when couples keep repeating the same patterns, especially after we've already explored them in depth. But this is where we must remember: insight does not equal change. Mental health systems need time, safety, and repetition to rewire. If we grow impatient, couples will mirror our frustration and assume they're failing us as well as each other. But if we stay steady, validating their effort while gently holding them accountable, they begin to internalise that steadiness.

There's a paradox here: conscious incompetence feels like the lowest point, but it is actually the beginning of transformation. The very pain of seeing the pattern without yet changing it creates the motivation to keep going. Couples who can survive this stage with compassion for themselves are the ones most likely to thrive long-term. Those who interpret it as failure often give up too soon. Our role is to help them hold steady, to remind them that awareness is progress, and to frame mistakes as stepping stones.

So while conscious incompetence feels heavy, it is profoundly hopeful. It means the couple is no longer fighting blind. They can see the patterns, even if they can't yet break them. They are awake to their own part in the cycle, even if they stumble in trying to change it. That is not failure. That is the messy middle of growth.

If conscious incompetence feels like the weight of knowing but not yet doing, conscious competence is the delicate stage where couples begin to practise new ways of relating with intentional effort. It is deliberate, sometimes awkward, and rarely smooth, but it represents a turning point. This is where awareness begins to translate into action, where partners start catching themselves mid-pattern and trying something different.

At this stage, couples often sound like learners rehearsing their lines. One partner pauses mid-argument and says carefully, "Okay, I'm trying to listen now, even though I want to interrupt." Or they say, "I'm going to try and say this in a way that's helpful, not unhelpful." It can look stilted, almost artificial. Sometimes they laugh at themselves, embarrassed by how clunky it feels. And that's the point: it's not yet natural. Conscious competence requires attention, practice, and courage.

From a mental health perspective, this stage is both stabilising and vulnerable. On one hand, couples begin to feel the relief of change. They notice that arguments de-escalate more quickly, that validation lands more often, that shame doesn't dominate every interaction. On the other hand, the effort required can feel exhausting. For someone living with anxiety, practising calm responses can feel like holding back a tidal wave. For someone with depression, mustering the energy to stay engaged can be draining. For trauma survivors, deliberately overriding survival instincts — speaking instead of shutting down, pausing instead of lashing out — can feel almost impossible at first.

This is why progress here often comes in fits and starts. A couple might leave a session feeling hopeful because they successfully paused during a disagreement. Then, two nights later, a stressful day leads them right back into old patterns. They return to counselling discouraged, saying, "We thought we'd cracked it, but we're back to square one." The truth is, they're not back at the start. They are learning to wobble forward, like toddlers finding their feet. Falling down doesn't erase the fact that walking is possible. It is part of how walking is learned.

I worked with a couple — let's call them Mia and James — who were deep in this stage. Their pattern had always been rapid escalation: small disagreements about money spiralled into shouting within minutes. After several sessions, they began practising a pause technique. During one heated exchange about bills, James stopped mid-sentence, put his hand on the table, and said, "Pause. I'm angry, but I'm going to try to listen." Mia blinked in surprise and, after a beat, responded with, "Okay. I'll try too." They stumbled through the conversation, but they avoided shouting. When they described it later, they laughed, admitting it felt staged. But the pride in their eyes was unmistakable. That deliberate effort, however clumsy, was a breakthrough.

This is conscious competence in action. The couple still feels the pull of old patterns, but they now have enough awareness and enough skill to intervene. And each time they succeed, even imperfectly, they carve new neural pathways. The brain is plastic. The nervous system adapts. Every time a couple chooses validation over criticism, pause over reaction, curiosity over assumption, they are rewiring not just their relationship but their mental health. Anxiety learns that danger is not inevitable. Depression learns that hope is justified. Trauma learns that new responses are possible.

It's important to acknowledge here that conscious competence can feel frustrating precisely because it requires so much effort. Couples sometimes say, "Why does this feel so hard? Shouldn't it be easier by now?" The answer is no — not yet. Like learning to drive, the early months are exhausting because every action is deliberate. Mirror, signal, manoeuvre. Check the blind spot. Adjust the clutch. It's not until much later that the body remembers without thinking. Couples in this stage are learning their equivalent of mirror-signal-manoeuvre. They're practising new habits of language, tone, timing, and empathy. It is supposed to feel like work.

Humour can play an important role here. Couples who can laugh gently at their own clumsiness appear to relax more. I sometimes encourage them to name their efforts with lightness. One couple began calling their attempts at pausing "the slow-motion game." Another referred to their validation attempts as "training wheels." These playful framings reduce the weight of shame and remind partners that learning doesn't have to be grim. Laughter in this stage is not avoidance; it's resilience. It shows that the couple is flexible enough to stumble without crumbling.

There is also a relational intimacy that begins to re-emerge here. When couples deliberately practise empathy, they often rediscover moments of tenderness. A partner says, "I can see you're tired, and I want to help," and the other's eyes start to mist. Not because the sentence was eloquent, but because it was intentional. Effort itself is healing. For clients who have lived under the weight of shame, seeing their partner try is often more powerful than hearing them succeed. The message is: "You're worth the effort." That affirmation is profoundly regulating for mental health.

Of course, setbacks are inevitable. Couples sometimes revert to old patterns, and the shame roars back. "We'll never get this right." In these moments, counsellors can act as archivists of progress. We remind couples of what they've already achieved. "Last time, you paused for five minutes before escalating. That's longer than before. That matters." Progress at this stage is measured in increments. Longer pauses, softer tones, shorter arguments, quicker recoveries. Each small step is evidence of growth, even if the couple can't see it through the fog of self-criticism.

Another key part of conscious competence is mutual accountability. Both partners must be willing to practise. If one makes the effort while the other clings to old habits, resentment grows. Part of our role as counsellors is to ensure the practice is shared, even if uneven. A partner who validates once while the other criticises twice is still progress, as long as both are in the game. The danger is when one partner weaponises awareness: "See, I'm trying, and you're not." That quickly pulls the couple back into shame and defensiveness. The antidote is reframing practice as collaboration, not competition. "We're learning together," rather than, "I'm doing better than you."

The mental health impact of conscious competence is profound. Couples begin to experience hope. Anxiety eases as partners see that change is possible. Depression lifts slightly as hopelessness gives way to pride. Trauma responses soften as the nervous system learns new options. These are not cures, but they are protective factors. They give couples a sense that the relationship can be a place of healing rather than harm.

I sometimes describe this stage as planting seedlings. The soil has been turned in conscious incompetence — messy, raw, exposed. Now, the seeds of new habits are planted. They are fragile, needing care and attention. They will wilt at times. Storms will come. But with nurture, they will take root. Couples don't yet have the shade of a full-grown tree, but they can see the shoots breaking through. That vision alone can sustain them through the hard work.

So conscious competence, while clumsy and effortful, is a hopeful stage. It is the bridge between seeing and being. Couples are no longer blind to their patterns, and they're no longer helpless in the face of them. They are learners, fumbling, practising, laughing, crying, but moving forward. And with each deliberate effort, they are not only growing their relationship — they are tending to their mental health, one intentional word, one pause, one act of validation at a time.

Unconscious competence is usually described as the final stage of learning: the point at which skills have become so embedded that they happen without effort. In everyday life, this is what allows us to drive a car without narrating every move, or to type on a keyboard without staring at each key. For couples, this stage can mean they've internalised new patterns of validation, empathy, and curiosity so well that they no longer have to think about them. They listen more naturally, validate more often, pause more easily. What once felt clunky and artificial now flows.

On the surface, this looks like the goal — and in many ways, it is. Couples who reach this stage often describe feeling calmer, closer, and more resilient. They can navigate daily stressors without collapsing into old cycles. A raised voice no longer triggers panic. A pause comes without conscious effort. Helpful language slips into place where criticism once ruled. It's a relief, and rightly so. This is the fruit of all the hard work that came before.

But here's where I add a note of caution: in relationships, particularly those shaped by mental health challenges, unconscious competence can become a double-edged sword. On the positive side, habits of empathy and validation now feel natural. On the negative side, slipping into autopilot can mean couples stop paying attention. They assume they've "got it" and grow complacent. The very awareness that protected them in earlier stages fades, and with it, the intentionality that made change possible.

I worked with a couple — let's call them Ben and Leila — who had made extraordinary progress. After months of deliberate practice, they reached a point where they were communicating calmly, validating each other regularly, and catching reactivity before it escalated. They described feeling more connected than they had in years. But six months later, they returned, discouraged. Old patterns had crept back in. Leila said, "We stopped doing the things we learned. We thought we didn't need them anymore." Ben admitted, "We got lazy. We just assumed it would keep working." Their story illustrates the risk: unconscious competence is not a permanent state. In relationships, stress, trauma triggers, and life transitions can quickly unravel even well-established habits.

From a mental health perspective, this matters because anxiety, depression, and trauma don't vanish simply because couples have learned new skills. They ebb and flow. A relapse of depression, a spike in anxiety, or an external crisis — job loss, illness, bereavement — can destabilise even the most competent couple. If they've drifted into autopilot, they may feel blindsided, asking, "Why are we back here again?" The truth is, they're not back at the start, but they do need to re-engage consciously. Without that re-engagement, shame can creep in, whispering, "We've failed."

This is why I encourage couples to treat competence not as a destination but as a practice. Relationships are dynamic, not static. Mental health is fluid, not fixed. Skills need to be revisited, refreshed, and re-applied. It's a bit like physical fitness. You don't reach a level of strength, stop exercising, and expect to stay strong forever. Maintenance is part of the process. The same is true here. Couples who understand this tend to weather setbacks better because they don't interpret them as failure. They see them as signals to tune back into the skills they already have.

For counsellors, the challenge is to balance celebration with caution. It's important to acknowledge the couple's progress — to say, "Look at how far you've come." But it's equally important to remind them that staying healthy requires ongoing awareness. I often frame it like this: "Competence in relationships is not about reaching autopilot. It's about having a toolkit you can access without panic when you need it. The fact that you don't have to think about it all the time is great, but don't stop noticing. Don't stop choosing."

Another metaphor I sometimes use is flying a plane. Pilots reach unconscious competence in handling controls, but they never stop paying attention to the instruments, the weather, or the runway ahead. They may not consciously think about every muscle movement, but they remain alert. Relationships are similar. You don't need to analyse every conversation, but you do need to stay attentive to the climate between you. Ignoring the dashboard is dangerous, no matter how skilled you are.

Unconscious competence also carries a relational risk: partners may begin to assume they know each other so well that they stop asking questions. Curiosity fades. "I already know what you'll say" replaces "Tell me what this means for you." In the short term, this looks like harmony. In the long term, it breeds stagnation. People change. Mental health changes. Stressors shift. A couple that assumes static knowledge risks missing the evolving needs of their relationship. Curiosity is not a phase; it is a lifelong practice.

This is why I sometimes encourage couples to revisit earlier skills deliberately, even when things are going well. Practising pauses during low-stress conversations, naming helpful versus unhelpful language in playful contexts, checking in with each other's needs regularly — these rituals keep competence conscious. They prevent complacency. They remind the couple that relationships are not achievements to be ticked off but living systems to be nurtured.

From the mental health lens, this ongoing intentionality is crucial. Anxiety thrives when couples slip back into avoidance. Depression deepens when efforts feel pointless. Trauma re-emerges when old patterns are triggered without warning. Conscious attention to relational health acts as a buffer against these spirals. It doesn't prevent all setbacks, but it equips couples to recover more quickly. They know how to pause. They know how to validate. They know how to externalise the problem instead of blaming each other. And perhaps most importantly, they know that competence doesn't mean perfection.

I recall another couple — Sophie and Daniel — who highlighted this beautifully. They had been practising helpful language for months, and it had become natural. But one day, during a stressful week, Sophie snapped and said, "You never help me." Daniel, instead of collapsing into defensiveness, took a breath and said, "That didn't feel like our usual way of speaking. Can we try again?" Sophie immediately apologised, saying, "You're right. Let me rephrase: it would help me if you could do the school run tomorrow." The slip didn't unravel them because they had kept the practice alive. Their competence wasn't just automatic; it was conscious enough to catch themselves when they slipped. That's the sweet spot: skills that feel natural but remain intentional.

So how do couples stay in this sweet spot? Reflection helps. Couples who take time to look back on how they've changed are more likely to maintain progress. I often suggest simple check-ins: "What's one way we've improved?" or "What's one skill we don't want to lose?" These questions keep competence visible without making it burdensome. They also strengthen mental health by affirming progress. Depression in particular can cloud perception, convincing people that nothing has changed. Reflecting on growth is an antidote to that distortion.

Supervision for counsellors serves a similar function: it reminds us of how we've grown, even when we feel muddled. Couples need the same reminder. Without it, they risk interpreting every setback as evidence of failure. With it, they see setbacks as part of the rhythm of growth.

Ultimately, unconscious competence is not about perfection or permanence. It's about integration. Skills that once felt foreign now belong to the couple. They've moved from "What do we do?" to "This is who we are becoming." The key is to hold that identity lightly — proud of progress but humble enough to keep practising. Relationships shaped by mental health challenges will always require attention. There will be good days and bad days, times of ease and times of strain. Competence isn't about eliminating struggle. It's about having the resilience to face it together.

So yes, unconscious competence is a milestone worth celebrating. Couples who reach it should be proud. But they should also remember that growth in relationships is never finished. Competence is not a certificate you hang on the wall. It's a rhythm you return to, a practice you repeat, a journey you walk. And in the context of mental health, it's the ongoing commitment to choose empathy, curiosity, and validation — not just once, but again and again.

CHAPTER 6

BEING AUTHENTIC: REFLECTION & THE CLEARER MIRROR

One of the conversations my counsellor peers and I often fall into is about authenticity. Over coffee, in supervision groups, or between sessions, we'll ask each other: what does it really mean to be authentic as a counsellor? Where is the line between showing up as ourselves and showing up as "the professional"? It is a lively discussion because the tension is real. Training emphasises professionalism, ethics, and boundaries — all crucial, of course — but the unintended message can sometimes be that authenticity is risky. That to be professional is to be polished, detached, or clinical.

I take the opposite view. Authenticity is one of our greatest tools. Without it, the counselling room becomes a stage play, with counsellors performing "The Professional" while clients perform "The Troubled Couple." Nobody believes it, and nobody relaxes. When we are real — congruent, as Rogers called it — clients sense it immediately. They soften. They feel permission to be real too. Authenticity is not about spilling your life story, but about showing up as a human being who happens to have skills, training, and a genuine desire to help. It is about congruence between what we feel and what we show, which clients detect far more quickly than we sometimes give them credit for.

This has direct consequences for the mental health of the people sitting opposite us. Clients who carry shame have spent years, sometimes decades, hiding parts of themselves. They believe they are broken, unworthy, or too much. When they step into a counselling space and sense that the person across from them is also hiding behind a mask, it reinforces those beliefs. It tells them that performance is the only acceptable way to be in relationships. But when authenticity is present, something else happens. The masks in the room drop, just slightly, and shame loosens its grip. Clients begin to believe that they can risk showing up as they are — imperfect, messy, uncertain — and still be met with compassion. That single experience can be the first crack in the armour of shame.

For clients struggling with anxiety, authenticity communicates safety. They don't have to decode hidden meanings or fear that they are saying the wrong thing. They can trust that what they see is what they are getting, and that is stabilising for a nervous system already on high alert. For those living with depression, authenticity offers evidence that they matter enough for someone to show up honestly. It says: I am willing to be here as a human being with you, not just as a technician applying tools. For trauma survivors, authenticity can be profoundly regulating. Traumatic experiences often involve betrayal or masks — people who said one thing but did another. When a counsellor shows congruence, clients begin to learn that not everyone will betray them, that safe connection is possible. In every case, authenticity isn't a side issue. It is core mental health work.

One of the simplest ways authenticity shows itself is through humour. Relationships are serious business, yes, but they are also wonderfully absurd. I have lost count of the number of times I have watched couples fight tooth and nail over dishwasher stacking, bin placement, or the right way to load the boot of the car. These are not trivial to them — they are symbols, as we explored earlier — but they are also recognisably human. Sometimes, in those heated moments, a gentle touch of humour transforms the room. Not sarcasm, not ridicule, but lightness. A raised eyebrow, a small smile, a remark like, "It's amazing how much power a bin can hold in a marriage, isn't it?" Couples often laugh, not because the issue has ceased to matter, but because laughter reminds them they are not uniquely broken. Other people argue about bins too.

Humour in these moments becomes a pressure valve. It releases tension just enough for couples to breathe and reconnect. And when it is authentic — when it comes from genuine human amusement rather than a forced technique — it becomes an invitation to honesty. Clients with depression sometimes describe laughter in the counselling room as the first light they have seen in weeks. Clients with trauma often say that humour helps them stay present when the work feels too heavy. Laughter doesn't solve everything, but it makes the unbearable bearable. It regulates bodies, not just minds, and it communicates that even in the middle of conflict there is room for joy.

Reflection is another form of authenticity, though it is often misunderstood. Too often, new counsellors treat reflection as a dry academic exercise: writing notes, analysing interventions, critiquing themselves like examiners marking a test. Reflection, in my view, is curiosity turned inward. It is not about proving you are flawless but about noticing what really happened and how it landed — and doing so with kindness. It is asking yourself: what worked, what didn't, what surprised me, what made me laugh, where did I feel stuck, and why?

Clients benefit from reflection because it models a way of engaging with their own experience that is not harsh or punishing. Many clients come into counselling with an internal critic that never rests. Anxiety magnifies every misstep, depression interprets every struggle as failure, and trauma distorts every memory into danger. When counsellors model reflection with kindness and humour — "That metaphor didn't quite land, did it, let's try again" — clients see a different way to live with themselves. They discover that mistakes don't have to equal shame, that imperfection doesn't have to equal rejection.

I once came out of a session convinced I had stumbled. I had lost my thread, repeated myself, even given an example that seemed to fall flat. Later, when I reflected, I realised the couple had laughed more in that session than in any previous one. They left lighter, more connected. My imperfection had made me more relatable, and in that relatability, they had found safety. That is the power of reflection: it helps us see beyond our distorted self-judgement. For clients, that lesson can be lifesaving. Depression often convinces them that every failure is proof of worthlessness. Anxiety convinces them that every mistake is catastrophic. When they experience reflection done with kindness, they begin to internalise it. They start to reflect on themselves more gently too.

I sometimes talk about the counselling room as a hall of mirrors. Clients come in carrying distorted reflections of themselves, shaped by shame, trauma, or years of criticism. They look in their own mirrors and see "useless," "unlovable," "broken." Our task is not to hand them a new mirror that says "perfect," but to help them see a clearer reflection — one that recognises flaws yet also acknowledges worth. And we cannot do that if we are hiding behind our own mirrors of pretence.

Authenticity matters because it says: I am not a flawless mirror either. I am human, like you. But together, we can see more clearly. That message is profoundly regulating for clients' mental health. It validates their humanity while opening the possibility of change. It takes them out of the lonely loop of shame and into the shared human experience of imperfection.

Authenticity, humour, and reflection weave together here. They are not fancy techniques or bonus extras. They are the foundation of relational healing. They invite couples to stop performing, to stop hiding, and to risk being seen. And in that space, shame loosens, anxiety calms, depression softens, and trauma finds its voice. Authenticity is not just good practice; it is the heart of mental health in relationships.

Authenticity doesn't mean we let it all hang out in the counselling room. Boundaries matter. Clients aren't there to carry our burdens or hear our full autobiography. But neither are they served by a cardboard cut-out version of us, carefully edited and polished until there's no trace of a human being left. The art is in the balance. Too little authenticity, and we feel distant, clinical, and hard to connect with. Too much, and the session becomes about us instead of the couple. The sweet spot is where authenticity serves the therapeutic relationship, where showing something of our humanness opens a door for clients to explore theirs.

This is where the debate about self-disclosure often arises. My peers and I have circled this many times. Some counsellors feel comfortable offering snippets of their personal lives, saying things like, "I know what that's like, I've been there myself." Others are adamant that self-disclosure risks muddying the waters, blurring boundaries, and centring the counsellor instead of the client. I've found a middle ground that feels congruent for me. I rarely share direct personal details. Instead, I use metaphor or analogy as a kind of indirect self-disclosure. If a client is struggling with reactivity, I might say, "It can feel like your brain's an overprotective bodyguard, jumping in with fists raised even when there's no real danger."

That is me in there, my way of making sense of reactivity shaped by my own experiences, but it is delivered in a way that keeps the focus firmly on the client. The metaphor acts like a bridge. It reveals something of how I see the world, but it does so in service of helping the client understand themselves. For clients battling anxiety, metaphors can turn overwhelming reactions into something understandable, even manageable. For those living with depression, metaphors can puncture the fog and give them a picture that feels hopeful. For trauma survivors, metaphors can soften the intensity, providing distance without dismissal. These aren't just clever images. They are small acts of authenticity that serve mental health by turning chaos into clarity.

A couple once asked me directly, "Do you ever fight like this at home?" It was a tempting moment for disclosure. Instead, I smiled and said, "You know what? Every couple gets caught in loops. What matters isn't whether conflict happens, but how we handle it. Let's look at what's happening between the two of you right now." That answer was authentic. I didn't pretend to be immune to conflict, but I kept the spotlight where it belonged. The point wasn't my story, it was theirs. And that balance is crucial, because clients' mental health is best served when the focus remains on their experiences, not ours.

Authenticity also shows itself in the way we handle the room. If I stumble over words, I'll sometimes laugh and say, "That came out all wrong, let me try again." If a metaphor misses the mark, I'll own it. If the couple laughs at my hand gestures — which happens more often than you'd think — I'll laugh with them. These moments aren't mistakes to be hidden. They are opportunities to model congruence. Clients learn, without us saying it outright, that it's safe to stumble, safe to laugh, safe to be imperfect. In relationships where shame has been heavy, this can be revolutionary. Shame whispers to clients that every mistake confirms their worthlessness. When they see mistakes handled lightly, they learn that imperfection is survivable. That is mental health in practice.

Authenticity runs like a thread through everything. It shapes the way we validate: "That makes sense, and I can see how heavy that feels." It shapes the way we question: "I'm curious what this means for you." It shapes the way we reflect: "I noticed your shoulders dropped when you said that." When clients feel the thread of authenticity, they trust it. They know we're not performing a role. We're present, alive, and real with them. And that makes all the difference.

I remember a couple I'll call Ben and Maria. They arrived tense, arms crossed, ready for battle. Every question I asked was met with suspicion. Their answers were clipped, their eyes darting as though testing me: are you going to take sides, do you really get us, are you for real? Halfway through, I fumbled a phrase. I meant to say, "You're both feeling unheard," but what came out was, "You're both feeling unhinged." I caught myself, blushed, and laughed: "Well, that wasn't what I meant — although you both look like you needed a laugh." They burst out laughing too. The ice cracked. The session shifted. By the end, they were leaning forward, sharing more openly than they had in weeks.

That was authenticity in action — not because I planned it, but because I didn't cover it up. The mistake, owned and lightened with humour, became the turning point. Ben later said, "That's when I realised you weren't just ticking boxes. You were actually with us." Maria added, "I stopped worrying about what you might be thinking and just said what I needed to say." Their mental health shifted not because of a technique but because authenticity created safety.

Authenticity, then, isn't a single act. It's a way of being. It's the willingness to show up as human, to risk imperfection, to use language that feels real, and to allow laughter into serious spaces. Boundaries keep us safe, ethics keep us steady, but authenticity is what makes the whole process come alive. Couples struggling under the weight of shame, anxiety, or trauma don't need a performance.

They need presence. They need to feel that the person sitting with them is not playing a part but engaging with them fully. That experience alone begins to repair some of the damage mental health challenges have inflicted on their ability to trust.

When authenticity is present, couples learn by example. They start to mirror that same authenticity with each other. One partner risks saying, "I'm scared" instead of masking it with anger. The other risks admitting, "I don't know what to do" instead of hiding behind control. These shifts are the building blocks of healthier mental health in relationships. They don't just improve communication, they reshape the emotional climate of the relationship. And they start, not with clever techniques, but with authenticity.

Reflection isn't just a supervision requirement or a line in a training manual. It's the beating heart of authenticity. Without reflection, we risk becoming technicians — applying skills without asking what they mean, repeating interventions without considering whether they fit, drifting into autopilot instead of learning. Reflection keeps us alive in the work, awake to the moments that matter, and grounded in the reasons why the couple's story matters.

I like to think of reflection as curiosity turned inward. We ask clients questions all the time: what does that mean for you, what story are you telling yourself in that moment, what feelings live underneath that reaction? Reflection is when we turn those questions toward ourselves, not as self-punishment but as self-understanding. It is when we say: what did that moment stir in me, where did I connect most, where did I feel uncertain, where did I notice lightness?

And reflection doesn't need to be a grand exercise with journals and long reports. It happens in the humblest of places. Driving home after a session, I'll replay a fragment of dialogue, hearing it again in a way that wasn't possible in the immediacy of the moment. In the shower, a metaphor will bubble up uninvited, one that I wish I had tried in the room. On a walk, a client's expression will return to me, the slight lift of their shoulders when something landed, and I'll suddenly see the significance I missed earlier. These moments count. Reflection sneaks up on us, reminding us that learning and growth do not end when the session does.

In these everyday reflections, questions rise naturally. What worked? What didn't land the way I expected? Where did I feel most connected, and what allowed that connection? Where did I feel awkward or stuck? What made me laugh? Humour is worth reflecting on too. Some of the richest sessions I've had were not the ones that flowed seamlessly but the ones where laughter broke through the tension. That laughter didn't erase the seriousness of the issues but gave everyone a glimpse of humanity in the middle of the heaviness. Reflection asks us to notice that laughter matters, that humour itself is part of healing.

Reflection is not about harsh judgment. It is about noticing and learning with kindness. When I stumble, I try to treat myself the way I would treat a client. Of course you felt that, of course you tripped up, of course you lost your footing. You are human. What can you learn from it? That stance protects our own mental health as counsellors. Without it, reflection becomes rumination, the inner critic let loose. With kindness, reflection becomes growth.

Clients need reflection too, though they rarely come in thinking of it that way. Many arrive stuck in distorted self-perceptions. Shame is often the loudest voice in the room: I'm broken, I'm useless, I'm unlovable. They see themselves through warped mirrors, each one stretching or squashing their self-image until the distortion feels like truth. I sometimes use the metaphor of funhouse mirrors. In Australia, I talk about the Royal Show, where kids laugh at the mirrors that make them look seven feet tall or bend their bodies into impossible shapes. Internationally, people picture seaside carnivals or fairgrounds. It's funny when it's a game. It's devastating when it becomes the only mirror you've ever known.

That's what shame does. It convinces people that the distorted image is reality. A forgotten anniversary isn't just an oversight; in the funhouse mirror it becomes proof of worthlessness. A raised eyebrow isn't curiosity; in the distortion it becomes rejection. Depression, anxiety, and trauma all feed those mirrors. A depressed client looks in and sees only failure. An anxious client sees only danger. A trauma survivor sees only blame.

As counsellors, our task is to help them recognise the distortion, not by declaring, "You're wrong, you don't look like that," but by holding up a clearer mirror. One shaped by empathy, validation, and curiosity. When we reflect a clearer image back, clients begin to see something different.

I remember working with a client who constantly called herself a failure. Every mistake at work, every tense moment in her relationship, every tiny misstep reinforced that identity. In her mirror she was short, squashed, unworthy. Through reflection in session, I said, "I hear you calling yourself a failure, and I can see the weight of that. But when I look at you, I see someone who seems to be doing the best they can despite huge challenges." Her eyes filled with tears. It wasn't about persuading her she was brilliant. It was about offering a mirror that reflected her effort alongside her pain.

That simple phrase — you seem to be doing the best you can — has become one of my most consistent tools. It doesn't dismiss a client's struggle. It doesn't argue with their shame. It acknowledges humanity and effort. Most people have never heard those words spoken to them. To hear it, often for the first time, can be deeply healing. For the anxious, it lessens the fear of not measuring up. For the depressed, it softens the despair of uselessness. For those living with trauma, it says: you are more than what happened to you.

This too is authenticity. We can't hold up a clearer mirror if we're hiding behind a distorted one ourselves. If we pretend to be flawless, clients will never believe us when we tell them their distortions aren't the whole story. But when we're congruent — when we own our stumbles, our laughter, our humanity — clients see that clarity is possible. Reflection is not just for us, it becomes a model for them.

Reflection also means noticing how we appear in clients' mirrors. Sometimes, despite our best intentions, clients project distortion onto us. They'll say, "You think I'm pathetic," or "You're siding with him," or "You're judging me." Our instinct might be to deny it quickly: "No, I'm not." But reflection invites us to slow down. What's happening in their mirror right now? What past experience is shaping the way they see me? Responding with authenticity might sound like, "It seems like you felt judged just now. That matters. Can we look together at where that feeling comes from?" Rather than defending ourselves, we use the moment to deepen the work. The mirror metaphor helps both us and our clients see that what feels true isn't always the whole picture.

Reflection, humour, and authenticity belong together. Reflection keeps us learning, humour keeps us human, authenticity weaves the two into a way of being that clients can trust. When we reflect without humour, we risk being too harsh on ourselves. When we use humour without reflection, we risk being flippant. But when we bring them together — curious, kind, light but thoughtful — we model a different way of being human. Clients see that mistakes don't have to mean shame. They can mean growth.

That's the gift of authenticity. It's not about being perfect. It's about being real. And in a world full of distorted mirrors, realness — and simple phrases like, "You seem to be doing the best you can" — is one of the most healing things we can offer.

Authenticity, humour, and reflection don't just shape the way we work with clients. They also keep us steady as counsellors. This profession asks a lot of us. We sit with pain, frustration, trauma, shame, and conflict. If we try to meet that with a polished mask, pretending to be unshakable, we burn out quickly. Authenticity acts like a compass. It keeps us aligned with why we came into the work in the first place. When we show up as ourselves — imperfect but real — the job feels sustainable. We don't have to put on a costume every time we open the counselling room door. Clients aren't looking for an actor anyway. They're looking for a human who can meet them in their struggle with honesty and compassion.

Reflection is how we check the compass. Driving home, walking, or standing under hot water in the shower, we take stock. Am I staying true to myself? Am I showing up with empathy, or am I slipping into performance? Am I being the kind of counsellor I would want to sit with? These quiet questions help us notice drift before it becomes distance. Without reflection, the danger isn't just professional drift — it's mental health erosion, both for counsellor and client. Without reflection, our responses risk becoming rote, our empathy mechanical, and our interventions hollow. Reflection keeps us alive to the living, breathing humans in front of us.

Humour is the fuel that keeps us going. Without it, the work can feel unbearably heavy. I've found that a well-timed chuckle in session is just as important for me as it is for the clients. It's a reminder that even in the middle of serious conversations, humanity has space for lightness. I once spoke with a colleague who admitted she felt guilty for laughing in sessions, as though humour undermined the gravity of the work. I asked her to reflect on when clients laughed with her. She realised those were often the moments they felt closest, safest, most connected. Humour hadn't diluted the work — it had deepened it.

That's the paradox. Authenticity doesn't weaken professionalism. It strengthens it. Reflection doesn't make us self-absorbed. It makes us better at noticing. Humour doesn't trivialise. It humanises. Together, they form a resilient way of working that can carry us for years without hardening or burning out. And that has direct consequences for the mental health of clients. Couples sense when the person in the chair is alive to them, not weighed down by masks. They lean in when they see congruence. They soften when humour tells them the weight they're carrying doesn't make them alien. They trust more deeply when they sense the counsellor reflects honestly rather than performing.

Clients notice. They notice when we're being real. They notice when we're curious about ourselves as well as them. They notice when we allow laughter to ease the tension. Those qualities don't just help them trust us — they model new ways of being for them. A couple once said to me at the end of a particularly tough session, "You made this feel possible. Not because you had the answers, but because you didn't pretend it was easy for you either." That was authenticity at work. Not polished brilliance, but honest presence.

Authenticity is also about resilience in the face of our own mistakes. There will always be sessions where I walk out thinking, "That was clunky." Reflection softens the judgement: yes, it was clunky, and that means you were trying something new. Humour helps me smile at myself rather than spiral into criticism. Authenticity reminds me that clients don't need a flawless counsellor. They need a real one. This matters for their mental health because many clients live under the tyranny of perfectionism. When they see us embody imperfection without collapse, they learn a different way of being. They see that stumbling doesn't equal failure. It equals learning.

This doesn't mean dropping boundaries or turning the work into stand-up comedy. It means being congruent. It means speaking in language that feels natural, noticing when shame distorts the mirror, and being willing to say, "You seem to be doing the best you can." That phrase, simple as it is, has the power to recalibrate the way clients see themselves. For some, it is the first time they have ever heard that their effort counts, that their humanity is enough. For clients battling depression, those words can break through the fog of worthlessness. For anxious clients, they can quieten the internal critic that never rests. For couples weighed down by shame, they can reset the entire atmosphere of the relationship.

Authenticity also serves as a protective factor. When sessions get heavy — and they will — it's our authenticity that stops us from getting swallowed by the darkness. Because when we're grounded in who we are, we can sit with pain without losing ourselves in it. Reflection helps us notice when we're carrying too much. Humour helps us release some of it. Together, they keep us from burning out. This isn't just about counsellor wellbeing. Burnt-out counsellors inadvertently pass the weight onto clients, creating distance where connection should be. Authenticity, reflection, and humour keep us present enough to do the work that matters.

For counsellors early in their career, all of this can feel daunting. You're told to uphold boundaries, maintain professionalism, follow ethics codes, document meticulously. All of that is important. But don't forget: you're also allowed to be human. To smile, to laugh, to trip over your words, to reflect while you're driving home. Clients don't remember every technique we used. They remember how they felt in the room with us. Did they feel judged or understood? Dismissed or validated? Alone or accompanied? Authenticity, humour, and reflection shape those answers more than any model or manual.

So when you wonder how much of yourself you can bring into the room, remember this: bring enough that clients can see you're real, but not so much that it becomes about you. Share your humanity, but always in service of theirs. Use humour as a bridge, not a shield. Reflect often, kindly, and curiously. Keep showing up as the kind of counsellor who can say with honesty, "You seem to be doing the best you can." Because in the end, that's what most clients need to hear — and what most counsellors need to remember.

CHAPTER 7

THE POWER OF THE PAUSE: CREATING SPACE FOR CHANGE

One of the most underrated skills in relationships—and in counselling—is the ability to pause. It sounds simple: stop, breathe, wait before reacting. But in practice, the pause is often the hardest skill of all. Most couples don't pause. They react. A word stings, a look triggers, a memory flares, and before they know it, they're halfway through an argument they never meant to have. The dishwasher, the phone, the bins—they all become accelerants thrown onto the fire. Pausing interrupts the chain. It cuts the fuse. It creates space between the trigger and the reaction. And in that space, something different can happen.

Viktor Frankl, the psychiatrist and Holocaust survivor, put it like this: "Between stimulus and response there is a space. In that space is our power to choose our response. In our response lies our growth and our freedom." That's what the pause is: the space where choice lives. Without it, we run on autopilot, repeating the same patterns. With it, we gain the freedom to step off the hamster wheel and try a new path.

For counsellors, teaching the pause is both simple and profound. Simple, because it often starts with nothing more than a breath. Profound, because that breath can shift the entire emotional climate of a relationship. I once worked with a couple, Liam and Hannah, who would go from zero to shouting in seconds. I asked them to practise pausing whenever they noticed themselves heating up. Not to solve the argument, not to walk away forever, but just to stop long enough to notice: "What's happening in me right now?" The first time they tried it, Liam admitted, "I paused, but only long enough to think of a better comeback." We laughed. That's normal. Pausing isn't about plotting your next attack. It's about noticing the surge and softening it before it spills over. By their fourth session, Hannah said, "I caught myself. I was about to snap, but I took a breath instead. It gave me just enough space to ask him what he meant instead of assuming." That's the pause in action.

I sometimes compare the pause to a speed bump. When you're driving, a speed bump forces you to slow down. You can ignore it and fly over, but you'll damage the car. Or you can ease off the accelerator, roll gently, and keep going without harm. Arguments are like that. Without speed bumps, couples accelerate straight into collisions. The pause is the speed bump that slows them down, protecting both the relationship and their sense of safety.

The pause doesn't always come naturally. For some, pausing feels like weakness: "If I don't defend myself immediately, I'll lose ground." For others, it feels like giving in: "If I stop, they'll think I'm wrong." That's why counsellors need to reframe the pause not as surrender, but as strength. It takes more courage to pause than to react. Pausing is not the absence of a response. It's the conscious choice of a better one.

Practice helps. Breath pauses—one slow inhale and a longer exhale before replying. Body check-ins—spotting clenched fists, tight jaws, racing hearts. Word holds—silently counting to three. Micro-breaks—saying, "I need a moment," and stepping outside for sixty seconds. None of these stop the conversation forever. They just create enough space for choice.

One of my favourite moments is when couples begin to laugh about their pauses. A client once told me, "We both paused at the same time. We just looked at each other, like two deer caught in headlights, and then cracked up laughing." That laughter did more to defuse the fight than any clever intervention. Humour again, working hand-in-hand with authenticity and reflection. The pause gave them space, humour filled it, and connection grew.

For us as counsellors, the pause is just as important. When a session feels stuck, when a client's words sting us, when we're tempted to jump in with a clever technique—pausing can be the wisest move. I often remind myself: silence isn't failure. Silence is space. And in that space, clients often find their own words.

Pausing isn't just a mindfulness trick; it's a way of shifting how we see ourselves in the web of relationships. Murray Bowen, the founder of family systems theory, talked about the difference between reacting and observing. To him, the capacity to pause and observe—rather than instantly react—sat at the heart of differentiation of self. When we're reactive, we fuse with the other person's emotional state. If they're angry, we flare up too. If they're anxious, we scramble to fix it. In that moment, we've lost our own centre. We're no longer choosing our response; we're borrowing theirs. Bowen's invitation was simple but radical: stand back enough to observe what's happening. Not detach completely—that's withdrawal—but hold onto yourself while noticing the emotional process. The pause is what makes that possible.

Reacting is ultimately taking responsibility for other people's thoughts, feelings, and behaviours. When your partner frowns, you rush to fix it. When they snap, you snap back. Their state becomes yours, as though you're responsible for managing both. Observation, by contrast, says: "Their feelings belong to them. My feelings belong to me. I can respond with care, but I don't have to absorb or control."

This shift from reaction to observation is where the pause does its best work. A breath. A moment. A choice. Suddenly, you're not carrying two people's emotional loads. You're standing on your own two feet, steady enough to offer empathy without losing yourself.

I sometimes joke with couples that reactivity is really just a game of "tit for tat, clackity clack." One partner takes a swing, the other swings back. Clack. Clack. Back and forth. Nobody's really listening—they're just waiting for their turn to send the ball flying. Couples usually laugh, because they see themselves instantly. "That's us," they admit. And once they can laugh about it, they can start to see how silly it is to keep the clacking going.

That's where Newton's cradle—the desk toy with its neat row of suspended metal spheres—comes in handy. Lift one ball and let it go, and the energy clacks through the row until the ball on the far side swings out. Back and forth, tit for tat, clackity clack. That's what reactivity looks like in a relationship. One criticises, the other defends. One withdraws, the other chases. One sighs, the other snaps. The energy keeps transferring, neither stopping because each reaction fuels the next. But here's the beauty: if just one person chooses to pause—if they stop lifting and releasing their ball—the whole chain of kinetic energy stops. The clacking quiets. The system calms. That's the power of the pause. It doesn't require both partners to get it right at once. If even one person chooses observation over reaction, the cycle begins to shift.

I once worked with a couple, Matt and Claire, who illustrated this perfectly. Matt was fiery, quick to criticise. Claire was quick to defend. Their sessions often felt like watching a Newton's cradle in motion—Matt's words flying, Claire's retorts smacking back, energy clattering between them. I coached Claire to try pausing the next time Matt lashed out. Not walking away in silence—that would have fuelled his criticism—but simply taking a breath, noticing her urge to defend, and saying, "I hear you're upset. Let me think about that before I respond." The first time she tried it, Matt stumbled. Without the energy bouncing back, he had nowhere to go. The clacking stopped. Later he admitted, "It threw me. I didn't know what to do. But it also made me calm down." That pause didn't solve everything, but it disrupted the tit for tat, clackity clack just enough to create space for something new.

For counsellors, Newton's cradle is a handy visual. Couples immediately recognise themselves in the clacking spheres. They laugh, sometimes uncomfortably, but they see the truth: "That's exactly what we do." And when they see it, they begin to believe they can choose differently. Teaching the pause through this metaphor makes it concrete. It's not abstract mindfulness or "just breathe." It's physics: energy keeps bouncing until someone chooses to stop.

Of course, pausing doesn't come easily. It feels counterintuitive. When someone criticises, our instinct is to defend. When someone withdraws, our instinct is to chase. To pause in that moment feels like giving up ground. That's why we remind couples that pausing isn't withdrawal. It's not sulking, shutting down, or avoiding. It's a conscious act of responsibility: "I'm going to manage my side of the pendulum. I'm going to hold onto myself long enough to choose what's helpful." In practice, this often looks clunky at first. A partner blurts out: "Okay, I'm pausing now!" We laugh about it together. The important part isn't elegance—it's intention. Even a clumsy pause is better than a perfect reaction.

As counsellors, we also practise what we preach. Sessions sometimes get heated. Couples look to us to take sides, to referee, to react. In those moments, we can model the pause. We can breathe, slow down, and say, "Let's hold on a second. What's happening here?" That simple intervention often shifts the temperature in the room. The pause teaches couples—and us—that we don't have to keep playing tit for tat, clackity clack. We can let the pendulum rest.

One of the reasons pausing feels so difficult is because our nervous systems don't like it. When something triggers us, the body leaps straight into survival mode. Fight, flight, freeze, or fawn—those ancient responses take over before thought has time to catch up. That's why a pause often feels impossible. A raised voice, a rolling eye, a slammed door—the body surges before the brain even knows what's happening. One moment you're calm, the next you're in a full-blown argument, swept along in the rhythm of tit for tat, clackity clack.

The pause interrupts this process. Even a few seconds of breathing or silence can shift the nervous system from survival mode into connection mode. It doesn't erase the feelings, but it slows them enough to create choice. I often tell couples that their nervous system is like an overenthusiastic smoke alarm. It goes off at the first sign of toast burning. The pause is like opening a window and fanning the smoke—not denying the alarm but calming it enough to stop the panic.

A couple I worked with, Zoe and Chris, were masters of nervous system hijack. Zoe's tone sharpened, Chris's fists clenched, and off they went into another loop. We practised pausing at the very first signs: the eye roll, the sigh, the hand clench. At first, Zoe would shout mid-argument, "I'm pausing now!" We laughed, because it sounded more like an announcement than a tool. But slowly, it shifted. Instead of escalating, Zoe would breathe and say, "Give me a second." Chris, surprised, would soften. That micro-break stopped their bodies from galloping into battle. The beauty of the pause is that it doesn't have to be long. Ten seconds is sometimes enough. What matters is the interruption—breaking the kinetic energy of clackity clack long enough for the nervous system to reset.

I sometimes use another metaphor here: the remote control. Life, and especially conflict, can feel like a film that's playing too fast. Before you know it, you're halfway through the argument scene again. But imagine you're holding a remote with a pause button. You don't have to fast-forward, rewind, or even stop the film altogether. You just press pause. The scene freezes. In that still frame, you can look around: "What's actually happening here? What am I feeling? What do I want to do next?" Couples love this metaphor, because most of us have had that experience of hitting pause on a remote to stop a film mid-scene. It's vivid. It's accessible. And it gives them permission to imagine themselves with that kind of power in their own living-room arguments.

For some, the pause button feels artificial at first. They say, "It's not natural to stop mid-argument." And they're right—it isn't natural. It's learned. But so is reactivity. We learned tit for tat, clackity clack somewhere along the line. If we can learn that, we can learn to pause. This is where practice comes in. I sometimes set couples homework: choose one small trigger and practise pausing. Not the biggest fights—start with the small ones. The bin bag left by the door. The forgotten text. The socks on the floor. Instead of clacking back, pause. Take a breath. Count to three. Imagine hitting the pause button. Notice your body. Then choose how to respond. The point isn't perfection. The point is practice.

One couple told me that their children caught on faster than they did. Mid-argument, their eight-year-old piped up, "Mum, Dad, press pause!" They laughed, embarrassed, but it broke the cycle. Sometimes humour does the work for us. That's another secret: the pause doesn't have to be solemn. In fact, laughter often makes it stick. I've had couples giggle their way through a pause, saying, "Okay, we're hitting the remote," and then collapsing into laughter. That humour was more healing than any lecture I could give.

For counsellors, pausing with clients can feel equally clunky at first. Sitting in silence when a session gets tense is uncomfortable. But the more we practise, the more natural it becomes. Silence is often the moment when something new surfaces. Clients who are used to tit for tat, clackity clack suddenly have a chance to hear themselves—and each other. I often remind myself in those moments: silence isn't emptiness. Silence is space. And space is where choice lives.

There are practical ways to embed the pause. Begin with body scanning: notice the earliest signs of activation—jaw, heart, chest heat. Anchor in the breath: longer out-breaths to invite calm. Try word holds: "one, two, three" before speaking. Use time-outs: step away for sixty seconds with a clear promise to return. Each is a small way of pressing the pause button before the pendulum clacks out of control. Couples often tell me later, "It felt awkward, but it worked." That's Stage Three of learning in the competency model: conscious competence. Clunky but effective. Over time, the pause becomes less of a performance and more of a practice. And once it becomes practice, the music of the relationship starts to shift.

The pause is deceptively simple. At its heart, it's nothing more than a breath, a moment, a beat in the conversation. But that small beat can change the entire rhythm of a relationship. Pausing gives space for empathy. When partners are locked in tit for tat, clackity clack, they're too busy preparing their next move to hear each other. A pause shifts the focus from "what I want to fire back" to "what's actually being said." It turns the volume down on reactivity so curiosity has a chance to be heard. Pausing also gives space for observation. Bowen would say it allows for differentiation—the ability to notice what belongs to me and what belongs to you. In the heat of reaction, those lines blur. The pause redraws them. It's the moment when one partner can say, "I see you're upset, but I don't have to absorb that as my own. I can stay steady while still caring." And above all, pausing gives space for choice. Without the pause, behaviour is automatic.

With it, behaviour becomes intentional. It's the difference between clattering along the pendulum and gently resting the ball in your hand.

A couple I worked with, Sarah and Tom, discovered this when we practised pausing mid-session. Sarah had just snapped, "You never listen." Tom's jaw tightened—I could see the comeback forming. I raised my hand: "Pause." He looked at me, exhaled, and stayed quiet. In that silence, Sarah's expression changed. She softened, then added quietly, "I just want to feel like I matter to you." If Tom had fired back, we never would have reached that moment. The pause created enough space for Sarah to move from attack to vulnerability. It turned a clack into connection.

For counsellors, modelling the pause is one of the most powerful interventions we have. When a session heats up, we don't need to leap into complex techniques. We can simply breathe, lean back, and wait. That silence tells the couple: we don't have to keep going like this. There's another way. Clients sometimes find silence unnerving at first. They rush to fill it. But when they learn to sit with it, the silence becomes fertile. Insights bloom in the gaps. One partner finally says what they've been holding back. The other hears themselves for the first time.

Not every pause is comfortable. Some couples misuse it as a weapon—storming out mid-argument, shutting down without returning. That's not pausing; that's avoidance. Part of our role is to teach the difference. A true pause is temporary, intentional, and accountable. It sounds like, "I need a moment to calm down. I'll come back in five minutes," or, "Let me take a breath before I respond," or, "Can we hold this for a second? I want to think about what you just said." The commitment to return makes the pause safe. It tells the other: "I'm stepping back, but not away."

When couples understand this, they stop expecting the pause to be a magic fix. It won't erase conflict or guarantee perfect communication. What it does is create micro-moments where a different choice becomes possible. Those choices—to validate instead of attack, to ask instead of assume, to soften instead of defend—are what change the relationship over time. The pause doesn't solve the problem; it creates the space in which solutions can grow.

As counsellors, it helps to keep a few reflections close: Do I model the pause in my own sessions, or do I rush to fill silence? Do I teach that pausing is strength, not weakness? Do I make room for humour, so pauses don't feel stiff or punitive? Do I clarify the difference between pausing and avoidance? Do I trust that small shifts—a single pause, a single breath—can lead to big changes?

In the end, the pause is about more than conflict management. It's about creating space for humanity. Couples often come to counselling feeling trapped in the endless loop of tit for tat, clackity clack. What they discover, with practice, is that they can stop the pendulum. They can hold onto themselves, stay steady, and choose differently. And when they do, arguments that once escalated into battles shrink into conversations that end with laughter. Tension softens into curiosity. Distance narrows into closeness. That's the power of the pause—a tiny act, repeated often, that opens the door to change.

CHAPTER 8

COMPASSION & SELF-LOVE: THE GENTLE ENGINES OF CHANGE

If there's one quality that transforms both counselling and relationships, it is compassion. Not the fluffy, sentimental kind often mistaken for pity, but the grounded compassion that says, "I see your struggle, and I choose to meet it with care." Compassion doesn't erase conflict, but it softens the edges. It makes it possible to stay in the room when shame says "run" or anger says "fight." Without compassion, the pause is just silence. With compassion, the pause becomes connection.

I often tell clients that compassion moves in two directions: outward and inward. Outward compassion is about meeting your partner's pain without absorbing it as your own. Inward compassion is about meeting your own pain without turning it into self-attack. Most couples I see are skilled at neither. Instead, they react to each other's pain as though it were contagious, or they punish themselves for their mistakes as though shame were the only way to grow. The result is two people caught in defensiveness, each blaming the other for a bruise they were already carrying inside.

Self-love is usually the ingredient that feels most foreign. Some clients hear the phrase and roll their eyes. They picture yoga posters and bubble baths, or they dismiss it as self-indulgence. But true self-love is much more robust. It is the ability to say, "I am flawed and still worthy. I make mistakes and still matter. I stumble, but I'm still doing the best I can." That last phrase is one I return to often. "You seem to be doing the best you can." It is a gentle antidote to shame, a reminder that effort matters even when outcomes falter. When clients begin to use that phrase for themselves, the shift is often profound.

I worked with a woman named Kate who criticised herself relentlessly. Every argument with her husband became proof that she was "a terrible wife." Every moment of stress with her children was evidence that she was "a terrible mother." Her mirror, to borrow from the metaphor we explored earlier, showed nothing but distortion. Through counselling, I encouraged her to practise a simple phrase whenever shame rose up: "I'm doing the best I can." At first, she spat the words out as if they tasted sour. She couldn't believe them, and in truth she didn't want to — shame had been her script for so long that it felt dangerous to speak otherwise. But over time, the sharp edges softened. One day she sat quietly and said with tears in her eyes, "I finally believe it. I'm not perfect, but I am doing my best." That moment didn't erase every argument in her marriage, but it transformed how she showed up in the relationship. With more compassion for herself, she had more compassion for her partner.

Compassion is contagious. When one partner treats themselves with kindness, it often spills into the relationship. A husband who softens his inner critic becomes gentler with his wife. A wife who stops punishing herself for mistakes stops punishing her husband for his. The atmosphere shifts. The pendulum slows. And here is the crucial point: compassion doesn't remove accountability. Self-love doesn't mean excusing harmful behaviour. If anything, it strengthens accountability, because shame paralyses while compassion mobilises. People who believe they are worthy are far more willing to take responsibility for change than those drowning in self-hatred.

This has direct implications for mental health. Shame corrodes self-esteem, fuels anxiety, and deepens depression. It convinces people they are unworthy of change, or that nothing they do will be good enough. Compassion, by contrast, builds resilience. It allows individuals to acknowledge mistakes without collapsing under them, and to face conflict without being defined by it. Couples who practise compassion develop a buffer against the mental health challenges that reactivity and shame exacerbate. Their nervous systems calm faster, their capacity for repair grows, and their sense of safety in the relationship strengthens.

As counsellors, our task is to model this balance. We don't excuse harmful behaviour, but we don't shame it either. We hold clients accountable with compassion: "I can see why you reacted that way — and I also see that it hurt your partner. Let's look at how you might do it differently." That combination — validation plus challenge, empathy plus responsibility — is what makes compassion such a powerful tool in the counselling room. It is congruence in action, what Rogers would call the willingness to meet clients as whole people, flawed and struggling but worthy of care.

Compassion and curiosity are close cousins. Compassion says, "I care." Curiosity says, "I wonder." Together, they form the gentle engines of change. Without them, counselling becomes cold problem-solving or endless blame-shuffling. With them, the room becomes a space where couples feel safe enough to grow. A client once told me, "This is the first place I've felt I don't have to defend myself all the time." That was compassion at work, woven together with curiosity. It was not about fixing every argument or silencing every shame spiral; it was about creating a climate where both partners felt safe enough to stay in the conversation.

When compassion takes root, even the most entrenched reactivity begins to shift. A pause becomes more than silence. It becomes an invitation: a breath that says, "I will stay with you, even when this is hard." And in that staying, couples rediscover the possibility of connection.

Murray Bowen's work on family systems theory has shaped so much of how we understand relationships. One of his key ideas was differentiation of self — the ability to stay connected to others while still holding onto a steady sense of who you are. At first glance, it might not sound like compassion, but in practice it is. Differentiation allows you to meet your partner's pain without collapsing into it. It allows you to listen with empathy without fusing so tightly that their emotions swallow your own. In short, differentiation creates the space where compassion can live and breathe.

When partners are poorly differentiated, compassion often gets tangled up with reactivity. One partner feels hurt, so the other reacts by trying to fix it, by defending themselves, or by attacking back. This is where shame cycles flourish. The hidden messages sound like: "If you're upset, I must be bad," or "If I'm hurting, you must be wrong." Both partners lose their footing and fall into spirals of blame, guilt, and resentment. Bowen's invitation was different: to hold onto yourself. To notice the pull of reactivity and instead choose steadiness. Compassion, in this sense, is not about dissolving into your partner's feelings, nor about armouring yourself against them. It's about standing on the balancing beam — steady enough to see both your own reality and theirs.

I often use the image of an oxygen mask from the plane safety card. Everyone knows the announcement: "Put your own mask on first before helping others." Couples smile when I bring it up, but they nod too. It lands because it makes sense. Without oxygen, you can't help anyone else. Without self-compassion, you can't offer compassion to your partner. Self-love is the oxygen mask. It says, "I'll breathe first so I can be present for you." Without it, attempts at compassion often turn into martyrdom, resentment, or burnout. With it, compassion becomes sustainable and nourishing.

I worked with a couple, Mark and Katrina, who were deeply enmeshed. When Mark was stressed at work, Katrina would crumble emotionally. When Katrina was anxious, Mark would spiral into panic with her. They described this as compassion — "We feel each other's pain so deeply" — but in reality it was fusion. Neither had space to stay steady, so both were swept into every storm. Their nervous systems were caught in constant hijack, stress feeding stress until even minor triggers felt like catastrophes. We worked together not only on pausing, but on differentiation. I encouraged them to practise a simple script: "I can see you're upset, and I care. I don't have to feel it for you, but I can be here with you."

It felt alien at first. Katrina said, "It seems cold to not feel it with him." But over time, they discovered that this kind of compassion was warmer, because it was sustainable. Instead of both drowning, one could stay steady enough to throw a rope. The impact on their mental health was profound. Their panic cycles slowed. Their sleep improved. The constant pressure in their chests eased. Compassion rooted in differentiation gave their nervous systems a chance to recover.

Compassion is often mistaken for rescuing. But rescuing assumes the other can't manage, and it robs them of agency. Compassion, grounded in differentiation, says, "I see your struggle. I believe in your capacity. And I will walk alongside you." That is why compassion breaks shame cycles. Shame says, "I'm failing, and now you must carry me." Reactivity says, "You're failing, and I must fight you." Compassion says, "We're both human, doing the best we can. Let's steady ourselves and move together."

I sometimes describe compassion as balm on raw skin. Imagine skin that has been rubbed raw; it stings at the slightest touch. Reactivity is like pouring vinegar on it, making the sting unbearable. Withdrawal is like ignoring it altogether, leaving the wound open to infection. Compassion is the balm. It doesn't deny the wound, and it doesn't make it disappear overnight. But it soothes. It protects. It makes healing possible. Clients often nod when I use this image because they know the sting of rawness. They've felt the vinegar of criticism and the cold neglect of withdrawal. What they've longed for, often without having the word for it, is balm.

I recall Mark reflecting after several sessions, "I always thought if I wasn't hurting with her, I wasn't really loving her. But now I see that when I stay steady, I actually help more." That was the turning point. He wasn't abandoning Katrina in her pain; he was finally strong enough to stand beside her instead of collapsing with her. Katrina said, "It feels lighter. I don't feel like I'm dragging you under with me anymore." That is the quiet strength of compassion with boundaries.

For counsellors, weaving Bowen's wisdom into compassion work means helping couples shift from fusion to differentiation. We notice when they are taking responsibility for their partner's feelings instead of their own. We invite them to practise staying steady while still showing care. We encourage empathy that doesn't collapse into rescue. And when the shame voice says, "If you're upset, it must be my fault," we help them replace it with, "You seem to be doing the best you can, and I'm here with you." These small shifts change the emotional climate of the relationship. Arguments stop being about whose shame is heavier and start becoming opportunities for steady connection.

One client once said to me, "I thought love meant never letting my partner feel pain." That's a common belief, but it is impossible. Pain is part of life, part of love, part of growth. Love, when rooted in compassion and differentiation, says instead, "I can't take your pain away, but I can stay present with you while you face it." That kind of love lasts. Not fusion, not avoidance, but compassion with boundaries — love that strengthens rather than erodes.

As counsellors, we model this too. Clients bring heavy stories, and we feel the pull to absorb them. If we're not careful, we take them home with us, and the weight becomes too much. Authenticity allows us to stay human in those moments. Reflection helps us notice when we're slipping into rescue. Compassion — for them and for ourselves — steadies the beam. It keeps us from drowning in the stories we hear, and it allows us to offer care without depletion.

This doesn't mean becoming detached professionals who never feel. Quite the opposite. It means holding onto ourselves so our care is real, not reactive. Compassion and self-love, in Bowen's terms, are acts of differentiation. They let us be "a self" while staying connected to others. They let couples face each other not as rescuers or opponents, but as two humans, steady enough to share the load. And when they practise this, the whole system calms. The pendulum slows. The tit for tat, clackity clack loses its momentum. What remains is connection, steadiness, and the quiet strength of compassion.

Compassion sounds like a lofty ideal, but in reality it is made up of very small things. Not grand gestures or sweeping declarations, but tiny acts of care repeated over time. They are often so ordinary they barely register, yet when strung together they shift the atmosphere of a relationship. Compassion grows less from fireworks than from steady candlelight.

I often encourage couples to look for micro-acts of care, the everyday gestures that communicate, "I see you, I care." It might be making a cup of tea for your partner before they ask, sending a text that says you were thinking of them, or picking up their favourite snack while shopping. It might be as simple as a shoulder squeeze when you walk past. These moments don't look dramatic, but their impact is cumulative. They weave a thread of kindness that partners can hold onto even in tense times. Many clients tell me that once they started noticing these small moments, they realised their relationship had far more compassion in it than they first believed — it just hadn't been named.

Language also plays a role in how compassion is practised. Words can be weapons without intending to be. Couples often slip into "you never" or "you always," without realising the sting those words carry. They drip vinegar onto skin already raw from shame. The alternative isn't sugar-coating or silencing honesty, but finding ways of speaking that are both truthful and gentle. Shifting from "You never listen" to "It would help me if you could hear me out" is subtle but powerful. Moving from "You're always so critical" to "I feel supported when you notice what I've done well" can transform how the message lands. Compassionate language doesn't eliminate conflict, but it invites openness rather than defensiveness.

Rituals of care are another way compassion takes root. These rituals don't need to be elaborate. A three-second hug when someone comes home, a shared cup of tea before bed, a walk together on a Sunday morning, or even remembering to say goodnight after an argument — these small habits create predictable moments of connection. They act like pegs in the ground when life's winds blow hard. Couples often tell me that when everything else feels chaotic, these rituals are the glue that helps them feel safe together. From a mental health perspective, predictability reduces anxiety and provides nervous systems with anchors of security.

I remember working with Alex and Simone, who were locked in cycles of criticism. Alex insisted Simone never noticed his efforts.

Simone argued that Alex never listened. Compassion felt almost impossible. We began small, with an exercise that required them to name one thing they appreciated about each other each day. At first the words were stilted: "Thanks for dinner." "Thanks for feeding the dog." But gradually the tone shifted. Simone admitted she felt lighter knowing she'd be seen for something. Alex said it made him notice the good instead of only the bad. Their entire relational system softened, not because their conflicts disappeared, but because compassion became visible in daily, ordinary ways.

As counsellors, we sometimes worry that suggesting compassion will sound preachy, as if we are wagging a finger and saying, "Be nice." That rarely works. Instead, I frame it as an experiment: "What's one small thing you could do this week to show you care?" Couples often return with stories that make them laugh: "I made him coffee and he almost fell over in shock." Humour helps cement the practice, making compassion playful rather than heavy.

It is equally important to focus on self-compassion. Many people treat themselves with more cruelty than they would ever inflict on their partner. They berate themselves for mistakes, criticise their appearance, dismiss their needs, and hold themselves to impossible standards. It is difficult to pour balm on someone else's rawness when your own skin is burning. I often encourage clients to practise speaking to themselves as kindly as they would to someone they love. For some, that means repeating the phrase, "I'm doing the best I can." At first it feels ridiculous, even embarrassing. But silliness itself can be healing, and over time the phrase softens into belief.

One client once told me she began saying it in the mirror each morning. The first week, she said it through clenched teeth, eyes rolling. By the third week, she noticed she was no longer bracing herself before speaking. By the sixth, she said the words brought a kind of calm she hadn't felt in years. That calm became a resource in her marriage; instead of lashing out when she felt criticised, she took a breath and remembered she was already doing her best. Her self-compassion spilled into compassion for her partner.

I sometimes use the term compassionate curiosity to describe this practice. Instead of berating yourself with questions like, "Why am I like this?" or "What's wrong with me?" compassionate curiosity asks, "What's happening for me right now?" That shift in tone makes all the difference. The first version is an attack; the second is an invitation. Many clients describe it as permission to breathe. From a mental health perspective, this reframe reduces shame-driven thinking and builds self-regulation.

Compassion is not abstract; it is practical and embodied. As counsellors, we can model it in the room. When a client stumbles over their words, we can smile and say, "Take your time." When a partner rolls their eyes, instead of reacting, we can ask warmly, "What's happening for you there?" Sometimes I will simply say, "You seem to be doing the best you can." Those words are not meant to absolve people of responsibility, but to remind them that effort matters. In many cases, it is the first time they have ever heard such kindness spoken to them.

The danger, of course, is overcomplicating compassion. Couples can already feel overwhelmed by the sheer number of skills and tools they are asked to practise. The beauty of compassion lies in its simplicity. It is a touch, a word, a pause, repeated consistently. Those small acts of care may not feel impressive, but over time they change the whole atmosphere of a relationship. Compassion doesn't mean avoiding conflict. It means entering conflict differently, with softer edges and steadier hearts. Even when the pendulum threatens to swing into tit for tat, clackity clack, compassion slows the rhythm and steadies the chain.

In the end, compassion is the balm that keeps shame from festering, the pause that gives space for empathy, and the thread that weaves safety into love. Couples who practise it daily discover they don't need grand gestures to heal. They need small, repeated moments of care, for each other and for themselves. And from those small moments, the possibility of lasting change grows.

Compassion and self-love can sound soft, even indulgent, to people who have lived much of their lives in survival mode. Many couples arrive in counselling hardened by years of stress, trauma, or disappointment. They have learned to grit their teeth and push through, convinced that change must be dramatic, disciplined, or punishing. When I suggest kindness — towards themselves and towards each other — they sometimes look at me as if I have missed the point. Surely softness cannot stand up to the weight of their pain. Surely love requires toughness, not gentleness. Yet compassion is not indulgence. Compassion is resilience.

Think about it. Harshness breaks people down. Shame paralyses. Criticism corrodes. Over time, these habits strip away hope and erode trust. Compassion, on the other hand, sustains. It steadies. It builds the emotional muscle that allows couples to keep showing up for one another when things get tough. The nervous system, once accustomed to bracing for attack, begins to recognise that safety is possible. Shame loses some of its bite when the balm of compassion is applied again and again. Couples who once flinched at each other's words discover they can remain present without breaking.

Bowen's idea of differentiation of self fits here. A differentiated person isn't cold or detached; they are steady. They are compassionate without being consumed, present without collapsing into the other's storm. They can say, "I care about you, but I don't have to drown with you." That kind of steadiness makes compassion resilient rather than fragile. It prevents compassion from turning into rescuing or martyrdom. Instead, it becomes a strength that allows couples to weather storms without losing themselves.

I once worked with a couple who described this shift beautifully after several weeks of practice. "We still argue," they admitted, "but it doesn't feel like we're tearing each other down anymore. It feels like we're fighting on the same team." That was compassion in motion. They hadn't stopped clashing, but the battles no longer felt destructive. The shift from opponents to teammates was the fruit of compassion.

Self-love plays a similar role. Without it, people burn out. They pour everything into their partner or children, leaving nothing for themselves. Resentment builds, exhaustion spreads, and the relationship becomes brittle. With self-love, individuals learn to set limits, rest when needed, and nurture their own needs so they can keep giving without collapse. The oxygen mask metaphor fits perfectly: without your own breath, you have nothing to offer. Many clients nod when I remind them of this image — they already know it is true, but guilt and conditioning have taught them to ignore it. Learning to claim their own oxygen is one of the most radical acts of compassion they can make.

Counsellors are not exempt from this truth. Compassion and self-love are not just tools we teach; they are practices we must live. Sitting with the pain of others day after day can be draining. Without self-compassion, counsellors risk compassion fatigue — the slow erosion of our ability to care. But when we treat ourselves with the same gentleness we encourage in clients, we stay steady, creative, and human in the room. I often remind myself of the phrase I use with clients: "You seem to be doing the best you can." After a tough session, instead of spiralling into self-criticism — "I should have done more" — I try to say, "I did my best with what I had in that moment." That small act of compassion keeps me grounded, preventing the creeping burnout that so often silences empathy.

Couples, too, begin to learn that compassion doesn't mean perfection. It doesn't mean never raising a voice, never feeling frustrated, never making mistakes. It means noticing the stumble and choosing to respond with care rather than condemnation. Katrina once told me after a session, "I snapped at Mark again. But instead of spiralling into guilt, I apologised and reminded myself that I'm learning." That was self-compassion in action. Mark, instead of leaping into defence, replied, "I know you're trying." That was outward compassion. Together, they turned what could have been another tit for tat, clackity clack into a moment of connection. Their argument did not vanish, but it became an opportunity to strengthen their bond rather than weaken it.

The paradox of compassion is that it doesn't make people weak; it makes them stronger. It doesn't encourage couples to avoid conflict; it equips them to face conflict with more honesty and less harm. It doesn't let people off the hook for their behaviour; it gives them the courage to take responsibility without collapsing under shame. Mental health thrives in that balance. Shame isolates, but compassion reconnects. Criticism immobilises, but compassion motivates. In this sense, compassion is not only a relational tool but a mental health intervention in itself.

In counselling I've noticed that the couples who thrived were not the ones who never argued. Every couple argues. The ones who flourished were those who learned to argue differently — with compassion in their tone, with pauses in their rhythm, with gentleness even in disagreement. They discovered that fights no longer had to end in emotional bruises. Instead, arguments became opportunities to see one another more clearly. That is what compassion makes possible.

For us as counsellors, this is the essence of what we offer. We are not handing out fairy-tale cures or promising a world without conflict. We are offering tools that are deceptively simple but profoundly transformative. Compassion and self-love may sound like soft engines, but they are engines nonetheless — steady, powerful, and capable of moving couples forward when nothing else seems to work.

When couples practise compassion consistently, the atmosphere changes. The pendulum of tit for tat, clackity clack slows. Shame cycles lose momentum. Reactivity begins to soften. What replaces them is not perfection, but humanity: two people, flawed but caring, stumbling yet steadying one another as they go. They learn that they are not defined by their mistakes, nor by the worst things they have said in anger. They are defined by the way they return to each other with compassion.

And perhaps the most powerful transformation is internal. When couples begin to see themselves with compassion — not as failures, but as humans doing the best they can — that is when true resilience is born. It is resilience that lasts beyond a single argument, beyond a season of stress, beyond the counselling room. Compassion becomes the steady rhythm that keeps them grounded, the breath that keeps them alive, the gentle force that carries them forward.

CHAPTER 9

TRUST & SAFETY: THE GROUND BENEATH CONNECTION

If curiosity is the compass, and compassion the engine, then trust is the ground beneath the whole journey. Without trust and safety, a relationship cannot thrive. It may limp along, but it cannot grow. Couples often arrive in counselling describing their problems in practical terms: money, sex, parenting, housework. But beneath those details is nearly always a deeper, unspoken question: "Can I trust you? Do I feel safe with you?"

Trust isn't only about fidelity, though affairs often bring couples into the room. It is broader than that. Trust is about whether I can count on you to show up when I reach out. Safety is about whether I can bring my vulnerable self into the relationship without fear of being mocked, dismissed, or attacked. Without those two foundations, the other skills we have talked about — pausing, reflecting, validating, practising compassion — don't have solid ground to stand on.

I once worked with a couple, Melissa and Dan, who argued constantly about chores. To an outsider, it looked like classic "who does what" bickering. But when we slowed down, Melissa admitted, "When he forgets to take the bin out, it's not about the bin. It's about whether he cares enough to notice what matters to me." For her, the bin was a litmus test of trust. If Dan couldn't be relied on for something small, how could she feel safe relying on him for the big things? Dan, for his part, felt that Melissa's sharp words were proof he could never get it right. That shame made him withdraw, which confirmed her fear that she couldn't trust him. The cycle was never really about bins. It was about the ground beneath them cracking.

Trust grows slowly and breaks quickly. That's what makes it so precious — and so fragile. Couples sometimes hope I can give them a quick fix for broken trust, but rebuilding it is slow work. It takes consistency, humility, and patience. I often use the metaphor of a garden path. Each reliable act — coming home when you say you will, answering a message, listening without judgement — lays a stone on the path. Over time, the path feels solid underfoot. But one betrayal — lying, dismissing, walking away when you promised to stay — pulls up a stone. Too many pulled stones, and the path collapses. Rebuilding means laying the stones again, one by one. It cannot be rushed, and it cannot be faked. Trust doesn't respond to declarations — "Trust me!" — it responds to action.

Safety is just as vital. Without safety, vulnerability becomes impossible. If every time I share a fear you laugh at me, I will stop sharing. If every time I cry, you roll your eyes, I will stop crying in front of you. Slowly, the relationship becomes a stage play where only the most acceptable parts are shown. In counselling, I see this often. One partner sits stiff, guarded, measured. The other looks at me and says, "See? They never open up." But when I ask gently, "What happens when they do?" the answer is often something like, "Well, I tell them not to be silly." No wonder the shutters are up. Safety isn't about whether vulnerability exists; it's about how vulnerability is received.

For counsellors, the first task is to create safety in the room. Couples watch us closely to see if it's safe to be real. If I roll my eyes, side with one partner, or rush to solutions, the trust is gone. But if I model acceptance, curiosity, and steadiness, the room itself becomes safe enough for honesty. Sometimes that means slowing the pace. A partner may want to unload years of grievances, but I'll pause and check: "Can your partner hear this right now, or do we need to build some safety first?" Just as a plant won't grow in poor soil, truths won't land in unsafe ground.

Trust and safety are not luxuries. They are the foundation. Without them, all the skills we've discussed — pausing, reflection, compassion — are just techniques. With them, those skills become transformative. Trust reassures the nervous system that it is safe enough to open. Safety tells shame that it does not need to take over. Together they steady the couple, allowing mental health to flourish where before there was only reactivity and fear.

Trust and safety aren't just "relationship extras." They are mental health essentials. Without them, the nervous system lives in a state of chronic alert. Partners stay braced, waiting for the next dismissal, the next criticism, the next withdrawal. That constant readiness isn't just uncomfortable — it's exhausting. Over time, it shows up as anxiety, irritability, poor sleep, or depression. This is why I tell couples that trust isn't only about love, it's about health. Safety isn't only about comfort, it's about survival.

Trust rarely shatters all at once. More often, it erodes through a steady drip of small breaks that add up over time. There are the micro-betrayals, like not keeping promises, "forgetting" important details, or offering an eye-roll instead of listening. Each one quietly sends the message: "You can't rely on me." There are dismissals, the shrugging off of a partner's worries, the casual "you're too sensitive." These chip away at emotional safety until the partner learns to keep quiet — or to shout louder. And then there is absence. Not always physical, but emotional. Being in the same room but not really present. Absence tells the nervous system: "You're alone."

When these patterns repeat, the body begins to treat the relationship itself as a threat. Psychologists sometimes call this relational trauma. It isn't always a single catastrophic event. More often, it's the slow erosion of trust until every interaction carries an edge of danger. The result is a partner who flinches before speaking, who second-guesses before sharing, whose body remains tense even in moments that should feel safe.

On the flip side, trust is one of the most powerful protectors of mental health. It calms the nervous system, lowers stress hormones, and helps people bounce back from difficulty. Research has shown that safe relationships support recovery from depression, reduce anxiety, and even aid physical healing. A reliable partner is not just a source of comfort; they are a buffer against the wear and tear of stress. This is why in counselling we don't just teach communication techniques. We help couples build trust as a mental health intervention.

I often compare trust to a bank account. Every small act of reliability is a deposit: turning up when you say you will, answering the phone, listening without judgement. Every betrayal or dismissal is a withdrawal. Couples in crisis often arrive overdrawn. The account is empty, sometimes even in debt. Rebuilding trust means making regular deposits, often without immediate returns. A partner who feels unsafe won't be convinced by one grand gesture, but they will soften when they see a hundred small ones. Just as financial debt breeds anxiety, relational debt erodes psychological safety. And just as financial security brings peace of mind, a healthy trust account allows couples to relax. They don't have to scrutinise every transaction because the reserves are already there.

I remember working with Leanne and Victor, whose marriage had become a minefield. Victor lived with depression, and Leanne, desperate to shake him out of it, would criticise him harshly. He withdrew further, and she in turn felt abandoned. What shifted their dynamic wasn't a clever technique but safety. In one session, Leanne turned to Victor and said, "I know you're struggling. I'm not going to shame you for that anymore. I want to sit with you, even when you're quiet." Victor told me later it was the first time in years he felt safe enough to bring his depression into the relationship without fear of attack. That moment didn't cure his depression, but it eased his isolation. Safety gave him space to breathe, and with it came the possibility of healing.

For us as counsellors, creating safety in the room is one of the most important tasks we have. The couple may have little trust outside, but in our presence, they can begin to practise. They can risk being heard without mockery, challenged without shaming, and held without being controlled. It's also where we keep an eye on the mental health beneath the conflict. If one or both partners are showing signs of trauma, anxiety, or depression, we don't frame it simply as "bad communication." We name it as mental health stress showing up in the relationship. That shift reduces blame and increases compassion. Instead of, "You're oversensitive," it becomes, "We're both carrying stress, and it's shaping how we relate."

Trust and safety also act as prevention. Couples often underestimate this. Just as exercise strengthens the body before illness strikes, trust strengthens the relationship before crises arrive. When life inevitably brings stress, loss, or illness, couples with trust and safety can withstand the storm. Those without it are more likely to collapse under the strain. I sometimes describe safety as the immune system of a relationship. Without it, every disagreement becomes an infection. With it, couples recover faster, and sometimes even come out stronger.

Trust and safety are not luxuries reserved for perfect marriages. They are the ground beneath connection and the soil in which mental health grows. Couples who invest in them are not only building happier relationships; they are also building calmer bodies, stronger minds, and more resilient futures.

If trust and safety are the ground beneath connection, then repair is the slow and deliberate work of laying stones until the ground feels solid again. The challenge is that couples often come to counselling wanting shortcuts: "How do we fix this quickly?" But there are no shortcuts. Trust is not rebuilt with a single promise or a single gesture. It is rebuilt through small, consistent actions repeated over time, until the nervous system learns again that it can rest.

John Gottman has written extensively about the importance of repair attempts — the little gestures that stop conflict from spiralling: a joke, a smile, an apology, even a sigh. These small bids matter. But when trust has been broken, repair requires more than stopping a row in its tracks. It requires a conscious, sustained rebuilding process. I often tell couples: repair is not about erasing the past. It is about building a present strong enough to hold the weight of the past without crumbling.

The first step is acknowledgement. Healing begins with honesty. Pretending a wound doesn't exist only drives it deeper. If trust has been broken by betrayal, lying, or emotional absence, the first step is to name it: "I hurt you. I see that. I regret it." Without this step, the partner who was hurt remains stuck in hypervigilance, scanning for the next blow. The second step is consistency. Trust doesn't return with one grand promise. It returns through dozens of small acts: showing up when you say you will, following through on commitments, listening without defence. These small actions are the bricks of rebuilding. The third step is transparency. Especially after affairs or secret-keeping, transparency can be essential. Sharing whereabouts, opening phones or accounts — not as a punishment or a life sentence, but as a stabiliser until safety is restored. And the fourth step is empathy. Saying, "I understand why you're hurt, and I care about that," is like balm on raw skin. Without empathy, consistency feels mechanical; with it, consistency feels healing. Finally, patience is needed. One of the hardest challenges for couples is tolerating the lag between consistent effort and the nervous system catching up. The partner who broke trust often says, "Haven't we moved past this yet?" But safety doesn't return on demand. It returns on biology's timeline.

I often describe trust-building as laying bricks. Each honest word, each kept promise, each gentle response is a brick on the wall of safety. It takes hundreds of bricks to build a wall high enough to feel secure. It only takes one reckless swing to knock down a section. Couples sometimes groan at this metaphor — "That sounds like hard work." And it is. But here's the paradox: once the wall is rebuilt with awareness, it is often stronger than before. Because this time it isn't built on assumption, but on intention.

Why do bricks matter so much? Because the nervous system is always scanning for danger. In a relationship with broken trust, the brain interprets even neutral events as threats: a late arrival means abandonment, a sigh means contempt, a forgotten text means betrayal. Each new brick — each act of reliability and care — calms that alarm. Over time, the brain begins to relax: "This is safe again." Without bricks, the alarm keeps ringing, fuelling anxiety, insomnia, or depression. With bricks, the body rests. That rest is mental health.

I worked once with a couple, Rosa and Michael, after Michael had an emotional affair. Rosa's trust was shattered. She checked his phone, monitored his emails, and still couldn't sleep at night. The turning point came when Michael stopped minimising and said plainly, "I broke your trust, and I regret it deeply." Rosa cried, not because the words erased the betrayal, but because she finally felt seen. From there, the work was consistency: daily check-ins, openness with his phone, no secret messages. At first Michael resisted, groaning about the effort, but over time he noticed something: "The more consistent I am, the calmer she becomes. And the calmer she is, the lighter I feel." It took

146

months, but eventually Rosa said, "I can breathe again." That was the moment safety returned.

As counsellors, we don't hand couples scripts for repair. We steady them through the process when their patience falters. We remind them that acknowledgement matters, that consistency matters, that nervous systems heal in their own time. We also normalise the struggle. I often tell couples, "You're not broken for finding this hard. Your nervous system is doing its job. Trust will come back as your body learns it's safe again." That reframing reduces shame and helps both partners stay the course.

There is a paradox at the heart of trust work: the partner who broke trust wants forgiveness quickly, while the partner who was hurt needs proof slowly. Our role is to bridge that gap with honesty and patience. Forgiveness is not an event; it is a process. Safety doesn't return with words; it returns with bricks. And when couples commit to laying those bricks, something remarkable happens. Sleep improves. Anxiety eases. Joy sneaks back in. Mental health strengthens, not because life suddenly becomes easy, but because the ground beneath the relationship is finally solid again.

When couples think about trust, they often imagine it as a yes-or-no question: either it exists or it doesn't. But in reality, trust and safety are living systems. They rise and fall, strengthen and weaken, depending on how they're nurtured. Our role as counsellors is to help couples see that trust isn't just about whether their relationship survives. It's about whether their minds and bodies can thrive. Trust and safety are mental health resources, not just relationship ideals.

When trust is present, resilience follows. The nervous system doesn't have to stay on guard, scanning for the next threat. That calm state allows space for rest, laughter, intimacy, and problem-solving. Couples in trusting relationships tend to sleep better, regulate stress hormones more easily, and recover faster from setbacks. Trust is not just a preference; it is a protective factor. Like exercise or good nutrition, it builds the reserves that carry people through storms. But when trust is absent, resilience erodes. A late reply, a forgotten chore, a small sigh can set off the nervous system like a fire alarm. Couples find themselves living in hypervigilance, and over time this constant activation can turn into anxiety, depression, or physical illness.

Safety works in the same way. Safe relationships act like a vaccine against despair. When someone feels emotionally safe, they are more likely to share fears, admit mistakes, and reach for comfort. Those moments, though small, are preventative care. They stop conflict from hardening into disconnection. Without safety, however, the smallest misunderstandings can grow unchecked. Arguments spiral, shame deepens, and hopelessness begins to creep in. I often describe safety as the immune system of a relationship. When it's strong, the couple can fight off stress and recover quickly. When it's weak, every disagreement feels like an infection, spreading faster than either partner can contain.

It's important to remember that trust and safety don't exist in a vacuum. They are always influenced by broader psychosocial stressors. Work pressures can erode patience until both partners feel brittle. Financial strain can amplify old fears: "Will you still want me if I can't provide?" Trauma history can keep the nervous system on high alert, making safety harder to establish. Even cultural scripts play a role, with some messages glorifying independence to the point that vulnerability looks like weakness. This is why addressing trust means looking beyond the couple's dynamic and seeing the wider frame. A couple may be fighting about closeness, but in the background there might be housing insecurity, health worries, or unresolved family wounds that make safety feel fragile.

I remember working with Talia and Ben, who came to counselling not in crisis but out of foresight. They wanted to strengthen their relationship before starting a family. Talia said, "We don't want to wait until we're drowning. We want to build safety now." Together we practised rituals of trust: daily check-ins, consistency between words and actions, gentle ways of ending conflict without damage. Over time, these habits became woven into the fabric of their relationship. Later, when Ben lost his job, they told me that the trust they had invested in made all the difference. Talia said, "We were stressed, of course, but I never doubted he was with me in it. That kept me from spiralling into panic." Their trust acted as a buffer, allowing them to face uncertainty without collapse. That's what prevention looks like: investment made earlier becoming resilience when life turns difficult.

As counsellors, we need to keep drawing the link between trust, safety, and mental health. This isn't just about teaching relationship skills. It's about supporting nervous systems, reducing chronic stress, and building resilience that extends far beyond the counselling room. Couples who learn to practise trust and safety are less likely to fall into the cycles of hyperarousal that lead to anxiety and depression. They are more likely to notice difficulties early, to seek help before the ground crumbles, and to support one another through hardship without burning out. Our work is not about grand fixes but about helping them lay small, steady stones — actions, words, gestures — until the path beneath them feels solid again.

Trust and safety are not optional extras. They are the soil in which connection grows and the shelter that protects mental health. Without them, couples remain locked in tit for tat, clackity clack, burning precious energy in cycles of reactivity. With them, the atmosphere shifts. There is steadiness, room for humour, space to breathe. When couples discover this, they realise trust is not only about love — it is about health, about having a foundation strong enough to carry them through life together, steadier and healthier than before.

CHAPTER 10

CONFLICT, STRESS & MENTAL HEALTH: MOVING FROM REACTIVITY TO REGULATION

Conflict is unavoidable in relationships. Two humans, with different histories, hopes, and habits, are bound to clash. The myth that "good couples don't argue" has done enormous damage. In reality, the healthiest couples aren't the ones who avoid conflict but the ones who learn to move through it without destroying each other in the process.

But unresolved or hostile conflict doesn't just harm relationships. It harms mental health. Chronic conflict keeps the nervous system stuck in fight-or-flight mode. Heart rates stay elevated, cortisol levels rise, sleep is disrupted, and over time this physiological stress bleeds into psychological symptoms: anxiety, irritability, low mood, even hopelessness. I've had clients come in saying, "I think I'm depressed," and of course we take that seriously. But as their story unfolds, it's often clear that what's fuelling their despair isn't just internal. It's the daily grind of conflict: the shouting match over dinner, the silent treatment at bedtime, the morning laced with contempt. Living in a state of constant relational tension is living in a state of chronic stress. No nervous system can thrive under those conditions.

Conflict becomes toxic when it slides into reactivity. One partner raises their voice, the other rolls their eyes, and before you know it, the Newton's cradle of tit for tat, clackity clack is in full swing. The nervous system is hijacked, and rational thought leaves the room. From a mental health perspective, what's happening here is important: reactivity fuses the couple's nervous systems in a storm of dysregulation. They're not thinking, they're surviving. That survival state, repeated over and over, wires itself in. It makes couples more likely to see threat where there is none, to assume criticism, to interpret neutrality as hostility. It's trauma on a micro-level — repeated stressors that scar the system.

The task is not to eliminate conflict, but to help couples regulate in the midst of it. Regulation means shifting from survival mode back into connection mode. That shift begins with awareness. I often invite couples to notice the physical signs of reactivity: the quickened breath, the clenched jaw, the hot flush in the chest. These are not random; they're the body saying: "Warning, danger ahead." Naming them helps couples see that their fight isn't just about words, it's about nervous systems colliding. Then comes the pause. We've explored pausing before, but here it becomes specific: a breath, a count to three, a step outside the room. In conflict, pausing is not withdrawal — it is detox, clearing away the smoke before it suffocates. And finally, there's compassion. Not the soft, pitying kind, but the grounded compassion that reframes the other person from enemy to teammate. Compassion interrupts the cycle by shifting the frame: "We're both humans in stress. Let's steady ourselves before we tear each other apart."

Conflict leaves residue. Even when the shouting stops and the door slams shut, the body doesn't instantly return to calm. The nervous system can stay revved for hours, sometimes days. Couples often tell me, "We argued on Saturday, but I was still rattled on Tuesday." That's not oversensitivity. That's physiology. I sometimes use the metaphor of conflict as second-hand smoke. Just as smoke lingers in curtains and carpets long after the cigarette is stubbed out, conflict lingers in the body and mind long after the words are spoken. The smell of it remains. You may not see it, but you breathe it in. This residue builds up. Couples living in constant tension are essentially marinating in conflict's second-hand smoke. And just as second-hand smoke harms physical health, unresolved conflict harms mental health.

When conflict is chronic, anxiety is a frequent outcome. The nervous system, unable to predict when the next blow-up will occur, stays on guard. This hypervigilance seeps into daily life. One partner flinches at the sound of keys in the door. Another rehearses arguments in their head all day at work. This mirrors trauma responses. The body is wired for survival, scanning constantly for danger. Over time, the anxiety becomes free-floating. Even neutral moments feel threatening. Clients describe it as "walking on eggshells" — a phrase almost universally recognised by anyone who's lived in chronic conflict. On the other side of the spectrum, conflict can lead to shutdown. When fights feel endless, some partners stop trying. They withdraw, detach, or sink into resignation. Depression often takes root here: the sense that nothing will ever change, that connection is lost, that life together is an exhausting treadmill. I've heard clients say things like, "It doesn't matter what I do, we'll just fight again," or "I feel like a ghost in my own home." That hopelessness is more than relational fatigue — it's a symptom of depression.

Conflict doesn't stay in the head. It shows up in the body: headaches, stomach pains, high blood pressure, sleep disturbances. These are the physical echoes of unresolved tension. From a psychosocial lens, these aren't random complaints. They are stress responses. The body holds the memory of conflict, and without regulation, that memory becomes chronic strain. I once worked with a couple, Tom and Elise, who argued most nights after work. Tom would come home exhausted, Elise would feel ignored, and the evening would unravel into accusations and defence. The fights weren't explosive, but they were relentless. By the time they came to me, Elise reported panic attacks on Sunday evenings, dreading the week ahead. Tom described feeling numb, dragging himself through the day, secretly Googling symptoms of depression. Both had headaches, both struggled to sleep, and both said, "We're just tired all the time." When I framed their conflict as a mental health issue rather than just a communication problem, their relief was visible. It was no longer about "Why can't we just get along?" but about "How do we protect our minds and bodies from harm?" That question opened a new path forward.

By the time couples reach counselling, many have tried "just talking it through" and discovered it doesn't work. They assume the problem is lack of willpower or love. But more often, the problem is regulation. Their nervous systems are so primed for conflict that even small disagreements feel overwhelming. The strategies that follow are not gimmicks — they are health practices, no different to exercise or diet. They soothe the nervous system, prevent trauma loops, and protect against depression and anxiety.

The body is the first to know when conflict is brewing. A clenched jaw, shallow breath, racing pulse — these are early warning signs. But many clients have learned to override them, ploughing straight into arguments while their nervous systems scream danger. In counselling, we slow this down. We ask: "What happens in your body when the tension rises?" By naming these cues, clients begin to separate sensation from story. Instead of "You're impossible," it becomes "I notice my chest tightening." This shift interrupts escalation and provides a pathway back to calm. Couples also practise structured pauses — a hand raised, a phrase like "time out." Not to brood or plan a counterattack, but to breathe, stretch, or journal. The science is clear: it takes at least 20 minutes for the body to recover from conflict's surge. Without that break, couples keep clashing with flooded nervous systems. With it, the nervous system recalibrates.

Repair attempts are another essential tool. They don't solve the conflict outright but soften the edges. A small joke, a gentle touch, an apology — these are bids for connection. They interrupt the nervous system's recording of the conflict as trauma. Similarly, rituals of grounding help couples anchor. A shared phrase, a hand squeeze, even a glass of water can serve as signals of safety. Rituals calm the nervous system by creating predictability, a known buffer against stress and trauma. And finally, reframing conflict itself: when couples believe that fighting means failure, they collapse into shame. But when they see conflict as inevitable yet manageable, they regain agency. Shame fuels depression; reframing fuels resilience.

I worked with Amira and Luke, whose conflicts often left Amira shaking and Luke storming out. Both were exhausted. We began with body awareness. In session, Amira placed her hand on her stomach and said, "It flips when he raises his voice." Luke admitted, "My jaw locks, and I can't think straight." Naming these cues softened their intensity. Next, we introduced the structured pause. At first, Luke grumbled: "Feels like running away." But after trying it, he admitted, "It's the only thing that keeps me from saying things I regret." Finally, we worked on repair attempts. One night, after a tense exchange, Amira said simply, "Same team, right?" Luke sighed, smiled, and said, "Same team." The fight fizzled. Months later, Amira reported fewer panic episodes. Luke said he was sleeping better. Their conflicts hadn't vanished, but their nervous systems were no longer being battered. Their mental health improved because regulation replaced reactivity.

Conflict is not only a relational challenge; it's a public health issue in miniature. The way couples fight has ripple effects on their children, workplaces, and communities. And more immediately, it has profound consequences for their own mental health. When couples learn to regulate conflict, they build resilience. The nervous system learns that disagreement does not equal danger. This is huge for mental health. Instead of every argument triggering anxiety or despair, couples develop confidence that they can weather storms and return to calm. Prevention is just as important as repair. Couples sometimes enter counselling only after years of corrosive conflict, when depression has set in, anxiety is entrenched, or trauma has been compounded. But conflict regulation is also prevention, no different to brushing and flossing. It doesn't stop bacteria from forming, but it prevents decay. Pausing, repairing, grounding — these don't erase disagreements, but they stop them from decaying into chronic stress.

Conflict also never happens in isolation. Financial strain, workplace pressure, trauma histories, cultural scripts — these shape the tone and intensity of arguments. If counsellors focus only on the immediate quarrel, they risk missing these deeper currents. But when we frame conflict as part of a larger psychosocial web, couples feel understood in context. Their arguments are no longer proof they're "bad at marriage," but signs they're stretched thin, under siege from stressors that affect mind and body alike.

Hannah and Raj are an example. They fought constantly about bills, parenting, even which way the cutlery should face in the dishwasher. Each session felt like déjà vu. But when we zoomed out, we discovered Raj was working two jobs and rarely sleeping. Hannah's mother was ill overseas, and she felt guilty for not being there. Their "dishwasher wars" weren't about utensils at all. They were symptoms of stress layered upon stress. Once we acknowledged the load they carried, the tone shifted. Instead of "We're hopeless," they began to say, "We're exhausted." That reframe created compassion, and compassion softened conflict.

This is the bigger picture: conflict will never vanish, nor should it. Disagreement is part of intimacy; it's how we learn and grow. But unmanaged conflict is corrosive. It eats away at safety, trust, and health. Regulated conflict, however, becomes a crucible for growth. Couples who learn to argue well don't just stay together — they thrive. Their mental health improves. Their resilience increases. They become better parents, colleagues, and community members. Conflict is inevitable. Reactivity is optional. Regulation is learnable. And when couples choose regulation, they are choosing not only peace in their home, but steadiness in their minds and health in their bodies.

CHAPTER 11

THE RIPPLE EFFECT: COUPLES, FAMILIES & MENTAL HEALTH

No relationship exists in a vacuum. When two people walk into the counselling room, they bring entire ecosystems with them: children and grandparents, workplaces and schools, neighbourhoods and cultural scripts. And just as a stone dropped in a pond sends rings across the surface, the way a couple relates sends ripples through every layer of their lives. That's why relationship counselling isn't merely about helping two people "get along." It's mental health work in the broadest sense. Conflict at home can fuel anxiety in a child; a lack of safety between partners can echo into a workplace as stress-related absence; compassion, trust, and regulation model healthier dynamics across generations.

Home is a child's first classroom. Children don't just witness arguments; they absorb the tone, the body language, and whether repair follows rupture. A child who sees parents come back together after a clash learns that disagreements are survivable; their nervous system encodes regulation as normal. A child who sees only shouting, contempt or stonewalling, learns that love is unsafe; their nervous system encodes vigilance or avoidance. Years later, that same child may sit across from us with anxiety, low mood, or difficulty sustaining intimacy — not because they are broken, but because their first classroom taught chaos. When parents learn to regulate conflict, they aren't simply helping themselves; they are shaping the mental health of the next generation.

Unresolved trauma rarely disappears; it travels. Bowen called this the multigenerational transmission process — patterns of anxiety, shame and conflict that echo down family lines. I once worked with Martin and Sienna, who were locked in battles over their teenage son. Beneath the rows lay two stories: Martin's father was authoritarian and harsh; Sienna's mother was absent and dismissive. Both were parenting reactively, pulled by ghosts. When they began to see their arguments not only as present disagreements but as echoes of old wounds, compassion surfaced. "I snap because I felt invisible as a child," Sienna said. "I shout because I was shouted at," Martin admitted. The session didn't magic anything away, but it reframed the task: this wasn't indulgence; it was generational repair. The work of this couple would ripple forward.

The ripples don't stop at the front door. People bring home into work and work into home because bodies and nervous systems don't keep tidy boundaries. I've lost count of clients who describe phantom fights replaying in their heads during meetings, or lying awake before an early shift after a tense evening. Sleep suffers; concentration fragments; errors creep in; resentment blooms. From a psychosocial perspective, performance isn't simply about grit; it's about relational health. A manager with a safe home base has more bandwidth to lead. A nurse whose partner validates her stress is steadier on the ward. A teacher who is met with kindness rather than contempt walks into school with more to give. Relationship health is workplace health, whether or not anyone names it that way.

Beyond workplaces lie communities and cultures. Households shaped by contempt and secrecy pass on fear. Households shaped by empathy, repair and honest boundaries pass on resilience. Culture matters. Some scripts discourage apology or vulnerability — "real men don't cry," "a good wife keeps quiet." Those lines may have protected someone once, but they corrode intimacy and mental health now. A man schooled never to show fear may erupt in anger or fall into depression. A woman told to keep the peace may swallow pain until it becomes panic. Our task isn't to sneer at culture; it's to notice the currents and how they shape distress. One client told me, almost in a whisper, "In my family, men never apologised — it would be shameful." When he risked apologising to his son after a harsh word, he expected ridicule. The boy hugged him and said, "I didn't know dads could say sorry." One act of repair shifted an intergenerational script.

Children, of course, don't always stand outside the couple's struggle. When tension rises, systems look for balance, and the easiest third point is often a child. Bowen called it triangulation: two in conflict pull a third into the field to stabilise anxiety. It can look like closeness — a parent confides in a child; a child steps in with jokes or a hug; sometimes a child develops symptoms that distract the adults from their own quarrel. But it places an impossible weight on young shoulders. They become peacekeeper, messenger, or emotional sponge. Anxiety climbs; play shrinks. Some develop headaches, tantrums or school refusal. Others grow careful and quiet, carrying guilt they can't name. None of that is a character flaw. It is simply too much, too soon.

I think often of Clare and Jason and their ten-year-old, Mia, who was having panic attacks before school. At first they described her as "sensitive" and "a worrier." Then it became clear: when her parents argued, Mia rushed in to stop it. Sometimes, after a fight, one of them would vent to her, "You're the only one who understands me." Her panic wasn't random; it was her nervous system buckling under triangulation. When Clare and Jason saw this, they were devastated. We named it without shame: "When tension is high, it's natural to look for relief. Children often step in without anyone planning it. The good news is we can change it." They began saying to Mia, "You don't need to fix us; that's our job." They worked on boundaries — adult issues with adults — and on their own regulation. Over time, Mia's panic eased. She didn't toughen up; she simply didn't have to hold her parents anymore.

Attachment thrives when homes feel secure. Security doesn't mean perfect parents; it means grown-ups who repair after rupture and allow children to be children. When young eyes witness arguments followed by repair, they learn that conflict is survivable; their bodies encode safety even in difficulty. When they are dragged into the fray — directly or by implication — their bodies encode danger. Instead of growing secure, they grow watchful.

The cultural layer can intensify all of this. I worked with Omar and Layla, who came from a community where marital struggle was treated as private — even shameful. "We can't tell anyone we're here," Layla said. "It would mean we've failed." "My dad always said, 'Never let anyone know you argue,'" Omar added. Secrecy meant pain had nowhere to go; it fermented. Omar's mood dropped; Layla grew anxious; both felt alone. We reframed their silence as a script designed to avoid shame, not as a personal weakness. "The script says 'hide'," I said gently. "But hiding doesn't heal. Honest, contained sharing does." Naming the script liberated them to speak truthfully to one another. In time, they noticed their children copying their new honesty: "I was cross, but I'm okay now." The ripple ran both ways.

If you widen the lens to a neighbourhood, you can see it there too. Where repair and steadiness are practised at home, classrooms feel calmer, teams steadier, streets friendlier. Where contempt and violence are practised, schools manage anxious children, workplaces lose focus, surgeries treat preventable stress, and faith communities carry silent grief. This is why the simple work of pausing, validating, and repairing can feel deceptively small — just two people in a room — and yet be anything but. One safer bond strengthens a fabric; one regulated conflict interrupts a loop that would otherwise spill into every adjacent space.

Because systems are always in motion, couples sometimes look to their children, their colleagues, or their community to take the strain. It's understandable. When the water is choppy, we all reach for the nearest rock. But our task in the room is to help the couple become that rock for themselves. Awareness helps: "We're about to pull our child into this; let's stop." Boundaries help: adult issues between adults, and if we slip, we repair with the child, "That wasn't fair to you." Strengthening the couple bond helps most: the steadier the two points, the less need for a third to steady them.

Holding this bigger picture as a counsellor can be energising and sobering. I'm never just meeting two people; I'm meeting their children's nervous systems, their teams at work, and the cultural lines they've inherited. I don't say, "Your row about the dishwasher is ruining civilisation." I say, "When you practise repair, you're teaching your children that conflict can be safe," or "The way you support each other under pressure will change how you show up tomorrow." People lean in when they feel part of something larger than self-protection; contribution often motivates where shame cannot.

All of this loops back to mental health. Triangulated children often present with anxiety or guilt; freed from the burden, they breathe and play again. Adults who carry conflict into the workplace present with burnout; steadier homes give back energy and focus. Communities that normalise secrecy carry shame; communities that normalise honest repair build wellbeing. This is why I insist that couples work isn't "just communication." It is mental health care. The nervous systems we help regulate are not isolated; they are nodal points in wider networks that can spread stability or stress across generations.

I think of Daniel and Priya, who arrived after years of near-constant conflict. Their two children were anxious; home was tense; Daniel's performance at work was slipping; Priya had headaches and bone-deep fatigue. Over months, they learnt to pause, repair, validate, and say what would be helpful instead of what was not. They didn't become conflict-free — no couple does — but they became regulated. The ripples were unmistakable. Teachers noticed their children were calmer and more focused. Daniel's manager commented on steadier energy. Priya said the headaches eased. When I reflected this back, Priya said, almost surprised, "I thought this was just about us. I didn't realise we were changing everything around us." That's the pond in real time.

The pond image stays with me because it is simple and true. Each interaction is a stone. Some stones send out rings of anxiety, shame and secrecy. Others send out rings of compassion, safety and trust. We aren't the ones throwing the stones; couples are. But we help them notice where each stone lands and what ripples follow. When we forget this, we risk shrinking counselling to symptom management — clever phrases and set pieces — instead of showing why it matters: that two people choosing steadiness changes the texture of a home, a classroom, a ward, a street.

At first glance, the scale of it can feel heavy, and that's precisely why our framing matters. The point isn't to pile on guilt — "Think of the children, think of your team" — but to offer hope: "Every repair you practise is a lesson in resilience for your child," "Every pause you take is a deposit in your own health and the health of those around you." Couples who feel shamed shut down; couples who feel their efforts contribute to something meaningful lean in.

When I settle at the end of a long day and think about this work, I remember that I am never only sitting with two people in a room. I am sitting with families, workplaces and communities. I am sitting with stories from the past and possibilities for the future. Relationships don't end at the edge of the couple; they ripple outward, shaping mental health across generations. Every pause, every repair, every act of compassion becomes more than a skill — it becomes a contribution. And when we hold that lens gently, couples begin to see themselves not as problems to be solved, but as sources of steadiness. The water clears. People breathe. And little by little, the pond becomes a place where life can thrive.

CHAPTER 12

COUNSELLOR SELF-CARE AS MENTAL HEALTH PRACTICE

Counselling is demanding work. Sitting with people's pain, holding their anxiety, absorbing the weight of their conflict — it leaves a mark. We may not walk out of sessions with visible bruises, but our nervous systems know what we've been through. The sigh after a tough session, the heaviness in the car, the dreams replaying a client's story — these are reminders that our work shapes us as much as we shape it.

That is why self-care is not indulgence. It is a professional necessity. Just as couples need safety and regulation, counsellors need practices that steady their own minds and bodies. Without them, compassion fatigue creeps in, boundaries blur, and our mental health frays. It is tempting to think that because we are "helpers," somehow we are immune. We aren't. In fact, we may be more vulnerable because we willingly open ourselves to the storms that others are desperate to escape.

One of the biggest risks in this profession is vicarious trauma — the emotional residue of listening to repeated stories of pain. We may not have lived what our clients lived, but our nervous systems respond as though we had. Over time, the body accumulates stress. Sleep suffers, irritability rises, our capacity to sit in silence shrinks. I learned this years ago in policing. Self-care wasn't even on the radar. We went to the pub, we made dark jokes, we stuffed it down. But unprocessed trauma doesn't disappear — it leaks. It shows up in health, in relationships, in the ability to stay present. When I later trained in counselling, I realised what I had carried then was vicarious trauma without a name. And the naming matters. Once we see our stress not as weakness but as a normal biological response to repeated exposure, we stop blaming ourselves for "not being tough enough." It isn't weakness. It is biology. And like any mental health issue, it requires care, not criticism.

Self-care also means understanding the difference between burnout and compassion fatigue. Burnout can happen in any job — emotional exhaustion, depersonalisation, a reduced sense of accomplishment. Compassion fatigue is more specific. It is the erosion of empathy itself, the dulling of the very thing that makes us effective. Burnout might be solved by a holiday. Compassion fatigue requires something deeper: reflection, supervision, boundaries, and sometimes reconnecting to purpose. Without this, counsellors risk becoming technicians instead of humans — present in body, absent in spirit.

I've learned that humour and humility are two of the best antidotes. Not the cruel, cynical humour that numbs, but the gentle laughter that reminds us we are human. Counselling is too weighty to carry with solemnity alone. If you can't smile at your own mistakes, you'll drown in them. Humility helps too. When we accept that we won't always get it right, that sometimes the most helpful thing we did was simply sit alongside someone, we free ourselves from the burden of perfection. Humour and humility loosen shame's grip and keep us connected to the humanity we share with our clients.

The truth is, self-care is less about grand gestures and more about disciplined routines. For me it often means walking, a coffee with friends, camping in the Australian bush, or even reflecting in the shower. For others it may be mindfulness, exercise, or simply closing the laptop when the day is done. What matters is consistency. Sporadic care doesn't balance regular exposure to distress. Just as we encourage clients to practise regulation daily, counsellors must commit to routines that steady them.

Supervision plays a crucial role here. It isn't just about ethics or case notes; it's a place to reflect, release, and recalibrate. Counsellors who skip supervision could burn out faster, not because they lack skill, but because they lack somewhere to lay the load down. I sometimes imagine a counsellor carrying an invisible backpack. After every session they tuck in more weight: a client's trauma, a couple's conflict, a teenager's panic. At first it feels manageable, but over time the backpack grows heavy. Without self-care, it never gets unpacked. But with supervision, humour, reflection, and rest, the load lightens. We carry on steadily, not staggering under the weight.

We cannot offer what we do not practise. If we want clients to value reflection, regulation, and compassion, we must model them ourselves. This is not self-indulgence; it's professional integrity. Self-care is not about avoiding stress but metabolising it — ensuring that the ripples we send out as counsellors are steady, not jagged.

It's tempting to think of self-care only as an individual practice — eat well, exercise, set boundaries. All of that matters. But counsellors do not thrive in isolation. Just as clients heal in relationship, counsellors sustain themselves through connection. Humour, community, and collective care are part of our mental health, as essential as any personal routine.

Humour especially is underrated. A laugh between colleagues after a hard day can release as much tension as an hour of yoga. Humour isn't about dismissing pain; it's about creating breathing space. I once heard a counsellor say, "If I lose my ability to laugh at myself, I'll drown in the work." That resonated. Humour protects us from despair. It activates the parasympathetic nervous system, lowers stress hormones, interrupts the accumulation of trauma. For counsellors, it isn't frivolous. It's hygiene.

But humour alone isn't enough. Counselling can be lonely work. We sit in quiet rooms, holding stories we can't casually share over dinner. Without community, counsellors risk becoming isolated containers of pain. Peer connection changes that. Whether formal supervision, informal coffee check-ins, or professional networks, community gives us a place to exhale. I've seen the difference between counsellors who have strong networks and those who don't. The isolated ones often burn out faster, not because they're less capable, but because they're carrying too much alone. Community normalises the struggles of the profession. It reduces shame. It reminds us we are not strange or weak, just human.

Supervision itself is a form of collective care. It offers safety, learning, and containment — a space where the counsellor's story matters too. I once caught up with two peers over coffee, and instead of talking about cases, we spoke about feelings. We admitted exhaustion, laughed about silly mistakes, shared tiny joys. When I walked out, I felt lighter, though nothing in my caseload had changed. What had shifted was my sense of being held. That is the power of collective care: it doesn't remove the weight, but it redistributes it.

Some counsellors lean on friends or partners instead, but this can create pressure. Friends may not understand, and we may feel guilty for unloading. That's why professional community is so vital. With colleagues, we don't have to translate. They know what it is to sit with trauma, to hold silence, to feel uncertainty. With them, we can simply be. Sustainable self-care requires both individual and collective practices. Journalling without connection leaves loneliness. Joking with colleagues without reflection leaves trauma unprocessed. The sweet spot is integration: boundaries, reflection, humour, community, supervision.

And here's the bigger picture: counsellor self-care ripples outward. Clients don't just hear our words; they feel our presence. A counsellor who is grounded, rested, and reflective carries a nervous system that says: "You are safe here." A counsellor who is brittle leaks tension into the room. Self-care isn't indulgence. It directly affects outcomes. A regulated counsellor co-regulates clients. An exhausted counsellor transmits exhaustion. Our nervous systems are part of the toolkit.

Clients also watch how we live. If we preach boundaries but answer emails at midnight, they see the disconnect. But if we practise what we encourage — breaks, laughter, reflection, supervision — we model mental health as lived practice. For clients who have never seen this before, it can be profoundly healing.

Self-care shapes professional culture too. When counsellors normalise reflection, boundaries, and supervision, the profession resists the old martyr script — that good counsellors sacrifice themselves endlessly. Instead, we create a culture of longevity, resilience, and authenticity. Burnt-out counsellors destabilise the profession; a culture of care protects its integrity.

And then there's the ripple into society. Counsellors who practise self-care subtly challenge cultural scripts that glorify overwork and neglect. In a world that equates worth with productivity, we model something different: that rest is responsible, that boundaries are compassionate, that humour belongs even in heavy places. I once mentioned to a client that I take a walk after sessions. They said, "So you don't just sit here being wise all the time?" We laughed, but the comment stayed with me. Many assume helpers are superhuman. When they see we're not, and that we care for ourselves so we can care for others, it reframes mental health as shared humanity, not stoic endurance.

A colleague once told me of a client who said, "You're the calmest person I know. When I sit here, I feel my body finally relax." That calm didn't come from magic words. It came from years of reflection, exercise, humour, and supervision. The client felt steadiness because the counsellor's self-care had created a nervous system strong enough to share. That is the ripple in action: one person's self-care becoming another's safety.

I remember a time when I was close to the edge myself. The sessions felt heavy, the backpack was full, and even my humour — usually the last thing to go — felt dimmed. So I packed up the car and went camping in the Australian bush. Out there, under the wide sky, I sat by the fire listening to nothing more dramatic than a kookaburra's laugh and the crackle of wood. No couples arguing, no urgent emails, no ticking clock. Just space. The silence felt foreign at first, like I had to detox from the constant chatter of other people's stories. But slowly, my own nervous system began to settle. The firelight flickered and I realised how long it had been since I'd felt that kind of steadiness in my bones. The backpack was still there — you can't erase what you've heard — but somehow it felt lighter. I wasn't carrying it alone anymore; the bush itself seemed to share the weight.

When I returned to sessions the following week, something had shifted. I noticed couples leaning in a little more, relaxing just a little faster. They felt my steadiness before I said a word. And it struck me again: this is why self-care matters. Not just for us, but for them. Our calm becomes their calm. Our restoration becomes their possibility.

Self-care is not a selfish retreat from the work; it is part of the work. It is what allows us to sit in the storm and hold space for others without being swept away ourselves. It is what lets us remind couples, by example, that rest and resilience are possible. And sometimes, all it takes is a walk, a coffee with peers, or a night under the stars to remember that steadiness is something we can cultivate and carry back into the counselling room.

CHAPTER 13

FROM SYMPTOMS TO CAUSES: REFRAMING COUPLES

By now, a thread will be obvious. Whether we've explored curiosity, observation, validation, pausing, compassion, trust, conflict regulation, ripples across systems, or counsellor self-care, the same idea keeps surfacing: symptoms are never the whole story. Couples rarely fight just about dishes, bills, or whose turn it is to take the bins out. Those are surface ripples. The deeper currents — trauma histories, shame, unmet needs, and wider psychosocial stressors — are where the real work lives. That is the reframe I hope you carry from this book: relationship counselling is not merely about smoothing arguments or teaching tidier communication; it is mental health work. It is about understanding how anxiety, depression, trauma, shame, and social pressures show up in the ways couples reach for, miss, and find each other.

It's easy to see why the symptom trap seduces us. A couple says, "We argue about money," and it feels energetic and practical to move straight to budgets, fair-share strategies, envelopes and apps. Another says, "We fight about the dishwasher," and a rota springs to mind. Those interventions can help for a while, but if the argument is rooted in the shame of poverty, the fear of insecurity, or the anxiety of not being heard, a spreadsheet won't soothe the nervous system. The weed grows back because the root was never touched. The trap feels good because it looks like progress; but unless we look at what the fight represents — humiliation, safety, fairness, belonging — the same pattern will return wearing a new mask.

A cause-focused stance asks different questions. Not "How do we stop this fight?" but "What does this fight mean to each of you?" Not "How do we divide chores?" but "What does fairness or recognition symbolise in your story?" We still offer practical tools, of course, but we hold them lightly and only in connection with deeper layers of meaning. We listen for anxiety — what each partner fears losing. We notice shame — where each carries a painful sense of "not enough." We name trauma echoes — the old wounds being replayed. And we place the couple inside their psychosocial context — work pressures, culture, class, health, family scripts, financial strain — the cross-winds that fan the sparks.

Curiosity is the compass that keeps us here. A curious counsellor doesn't rush to fix. They pause, lean in, and wonder: "Why does this matter so much?" Curiosity is gentle but powerful; it opens doors solutions cannot. It also protects us. When we replace the burden of fixing with the responsibility of asking, the work remains human and sustainable.

I think of the couple who arrived furious about cupboard doors. It sounded almost comic until we listened. For one, open cupboards meant chaos — a visceral reminder of a childhood where nothing was safe or predictable. For the other, being scolded for cupboards felt like being scolded for existing — an echo of relentless childhood criticism. Once seen, carpentry disappeared. The issues were safety and self-worth. Closing a cupboard became an act of care; and when slips happened, they repaired with tenderness instead of contempt. This is the shift from symptoms to causes: small issues reveal big truths, and arguments become doorways rather than dead-ends.

Hold the frame in mind: each skill we've explored carries mental health consequences. Curiosity steadies anxiety because being understood reduces threat. Validation interrupts shame by saying, "You make sense." The pause regulates trauma responses, creating a pocket of safety inside the storm. Compassion builds resilience; trust and safety quieten hypervigilance; conflict regulation protects against depressive collapse and somatic strain. And counsellor self-care means our nervous systems can co-regulate rather than leak fatigue. This is not incidental. Couples work is mental health care. When we treat it as such, our choices acquire weight: we are not merely tweaking talk; we are calming bodies, easing minds, and shifting generational weather.

So keep four reminders close as your practice deepens: don't be trapped by the symptom; stay curious about what the argument represents; hold a mental health lens, not a moral one; and protect your own wellbeing so you can keep protecting theirs. Not every session needs to become a deep excavation — sometimes a shared calendar is exactly what a couple needs. But even then, let practicalities sit inside the bigger question: am I only addressing the symptom, or am I helping them name the cause?

Metaphors have been our companions because imagery travels where defences block. They've helped us keep hold of depth without drowning anyone in jargon. The weeds and the roots remind us that chopping back behaviour without touching history ensures regrowth. The question beneath a budgeting row isn't always "how much" but "who matters?" The pendulum — that Newton's cradle, tit-for-tat, clackity clack — shows how reactivity transfers energy until someone chooses to hold their ball. When one person pauses, observes, and breathes, kinetic fury loses its momentum; the nervous system finds a ledge, anxiety eases, shame softens, trauma echoes fade to a hum. The pond and its ripples remind us that every interaction is a stone. Harshness ripples anxiety into children, teammates, and neighbours; compassion ripples steadiness just as far. The funhouse mirror teaches that shame distorts how clients see themselves; a clearer mirror — "You seem to be doing the best you can in hard circumstances" — is not flattery, it is regulation. And triangulation's hot potato shows what happens when couples toss their heat to a child; the parents' hands cool, but the child burns. Naming the potato gives parents a picture they can hold onto: "We almost tossed it just then — let's keep it between us."

Metaphors are not ornaments. They are nervous-system tools. They bypass argument and land in imagination; they make theory visible and choice possible. The weeds keep us under the soil, the pendulum keeps us noticing reaction, the pond keeps us systemic, the mirror keeps us kind, and the hot potato keeps children out of harm. Each points us away from the surface and towards the story beneath: what is being carried, what's being repeated, what longs to be retired.

None of this lands without the counsellor's stance. Techniques matter and metaphors help, but who we are in the room gives permission for depth. Clients sense quickly whether we are congruent or performing. Authenticity here is not autobiography; it's honest presence. If we pretend to be endlessly serene or all-knowing, clients feel judged or small. If we are human — able to smile at our own clunky phrase, able to say "let me try that again" — shame loosens its grip and safety grows. A regulated, real counsellor invites real stories, and real stories contain causes.

Curiosity then does its quiet work. Without it, we race back to scripts. With it, we ask, "What fear sits underneath this anger?" and "What would feeling considered look like for you?" Curiosity reframes failure as information: there is more to the story, let's find it. Humour rounds out the stance. Not mockery or cynicism, but lightness in heavy places — "Toothpaste wars, ancient as time" — the soft smile that lets a couple breathe. Humour doesn't trivialise pain; it makes courage possible. It lowers the heat, re-opens connection, and makes the next step walkable.

When authenticity, curiosity, and lightness blend, we stop hacking at weeds and start watering roots. I remember the toothpaste pair. He squeezed from the middle, she from the end; it had become a siege. A gentle joke unclenched their jaws. With space to wonder, we discovered order meant safety for her after a chaotic childhood, while for him the squeeze symbolised autonomy in a life that had felt controlled. Once causes were visible, negotiations stopped feeling like surrender and started feeling like care. The tube was never the point.

And so, woven together, the themes of this book arrive at a simple truth: relationships are not only about behaviour, they are about mental health. Symptoms are easy to spot: raised voices, slammed doors, sulks, messy kitchens, toothpaste, cupboard doors left open. Causes live deeper: shame that says "you're not enough," anxiety that scans for loss, trauma that echoes old danger, cultural scripts that punish vulnerability, psychosocial strain that frays everyone's patience. The work is not to deny symptoms but to let them be signposts. If we hold the courage to look beneath, healing can take root.

Perhaps you did pick this up hoping for a toolkit, and in one way you've got one: questions that invite meaning, metaphors that make things graspable, micro-skills that steady bodies and open minds, reframes that lift blame. But more than a set of techniques, I hope you've found a way of seeing. The lens is simple: couples counselling is mental health work. A pause is a nervous system reset. A validation is shame interruption. A clean repair is depression prevention. A moment of curiosity is a tiny trauma intervention. When you hold that lens, the ordinary work in an ordinary room becomes extraordinary.

Our role is not to fix clients or hand them ready-made solutions. It is to walk alongside, hold the mirror without distortion, shine a light on the roots, help them notice their pendulums, their weeds, their ponds, and their hot potatoes. Our stance — authentic, curious, compassionate, with a dose of humour — gives them the courage to look. We hold steady while they tremble. We remind them that conflict can be survivable, shame can soften, and safety can grow. And we tend to ourselves, because our bodies are part of the toolkit; reflection, supervision, boundaries, rest, and community are not luxuries but clinical responsibilities.

I think of the couple who said, months in, "We still argue, but it doesn't break us anymore." That, for me, is the heart of it — not conflict eradication but resilience; not symptom suppression but cause awareness. The gift isn't a stormless sea; it's a steadier boat. And the gift does not stop with them. It ripples to their children, their colleagues, their community — a quieter house, a clearer head at work, a gentler street.

If you take only one thing with you, let it be this: the fight is rarely about what it seems to be about. Look beneath. Assume there are roots, ripples, echoes, and scripts at play. Remember the images because they're easy to carry: weeds point to roots; pendulums show reactivity; ponds ripple outward; funhouse mirrors distort; hot potatoes burn children's hands. Each one tugs you back to causes when symptoms clamour for all the attention.

And if you've read this far, thank you. You've stayed with a book that's part toolkit, part narrative, part steady insistence on curiosity. I wrote it for counsellors who want to go deeper than "communication problems," who want to see the mental health forces shaping love. The real work lies ahead — in your rooms, with your clients, in your own reflection and supervision. Take the tools and metaphors; try them, adapt them, laugh when they flop, celebrate when they land. Let your practice be human on purpose.

So what now? Stay curious when symptoms present; lean towards causes. Practise authenticity; don't perform counselling. Use humour wisely to crack doors that shame has sealed. Care for yourself as an ethical act. Keep the mental health frame in focus: every session is not only about helping a relationship survive, it's about shaping bodies, minds, and ripples beyond the door. Your presence matters more than any script.

Counselling is both ordinary and extraordinary. Ordinary because it happens in everyday rooms with cups of tea and tissues and long sighs. Extraordinary because, in those rooms, lives tilt — shame loosens, safety grows, resilience thickens. Hold that paradox. Let it keep you humble and hopeful. And when you're overwhelmed, return to your compass. Ask, as you ask your clients, "What's really going on here? What's beneath the surface?" That question will keep you from drowning in symptoms and will always, always point you back to causes.

Because in the end, this is the art: not fixing, not performing, but staying human, curious, and compassionate enough to see what lies beneath — and to walk with people while they learn to see it too.

ABOUT THE AUTHOR

Oliver de Nicolai
BA, GradDipCouns, MCouns, M.A.C.A.
Practice Principal and Clinical Supervisor

Oliver de Nicolai is the practice principal and owner of Blue Healers Counselling, a skilled counsellor, registered clinical supervisor, and author whose diverse journey has profoundly shaped his approach to therapy. With over 15 years as a Police Officer in the Western Australia Police Force, combined with extensive experience in sales and consulting, Oliver possesses a unique blend of skills that enrich his ability to connect with clients from all walks of life.

His background in law enforcement has equipped him with invaluable skills in crisis management, trauma response, and conflict resolution. These experiences inform his compassionate approach, allowing him to create a safe and non-judgmental environment where clients feel empowered to share their stories. As an insightful listener, Oliver fosters moments of self-awareness and clarity that are essential for personal growth.

In his role as a clinical supervisor, Oliver is dedicated to guiding the next generation of counsellors, providing them with the support and mentorship needed to navigate the complexities of the field. He understands the transition from theory to practice and aims to inspire aspiring counsellors through this book, sharing practical insights and personal anecdotes that illuminate the path ahead.

Oliver is the author of *The Counsellor's Toolkit: From Law Enforcement to Counselling – Practical Advice for New Counsellors and Ideas for Career-Changing First Responders* and *The Counsellor's Toolkit: Metaphorically Speaking – A Counsellor's Guide to the Art of Metaphors*, both available on Amazon.

He is available for telehealth Australia wide or face to face in Brisbane Queensland, Australia for both counselling and clinical supervision. www.bluehealerscounselling.com.au